SCHIZOPHRENIA
AS A LIFE STYLE

About the Authors

Arthur Burton was formerly Professor of Psychology at the California State University, Sacramento, and now practices and teaches psychotherapy in that city. Dr. Burton, who earned his Ph.D. at the University of California, Berkeley, has published widely in professional journals and is the author of *Psychotherapy of the Psychoses* and *Modern Humanistic Psychotherapy,* among other volumes.

Juan J. Lopez-Ibor, M.D., Chairman of the Department of Psychiatry and Medical Psychology in the School of Medicine, University of Madrid, is Past President of the World Association of Psychiatry. He has published 15 books on psychiatry in Spanish and is a leading psychiatric authority in Hispanic countries. His speciality is schizophrenia.

Werner M. Mendel, M.D., is Professor of Psychiatry at the University of Southern California School of Medicine, Los Angeles, and a member of the Southern California Psychoanalytic Society. Dr. Mendel is the author of *Therapeutic Management of Psychological Illness* (with Gerald A. Green), as well as other publications.

Otto A. Will, Jr., M.D., is Medical Director of the Austen Riggs Center, Inc., Stockbridge, Massachusetts.

SCHIZOPHRENIA
AS A LIFE STYLE

ARTHUR BURTON
JUAN J. LOPEZ-IBOR
WERNER M. MENDEL

with a Foreword by
Otto A. Will, Jr.

SPRINGER PUBLISHING COMPANY, INC.
New York

SPRINGER PUBLISHING COMPANY, Inc.
200 Park Avenue South, New York, New York 10003

Library of Congress Catalog Card Number: 73–88105
International Standard Book Number: 0–8261–1570–5

74 75 76 77 78 / 10 9 8 7 6 5 4 3 2 1

Printed in U.S.A.

CONTENTS

FOREWORD

Otto A. Will, Jr.

This book is concerned with a collection of behaviors known as "schizophrenia," and as such may properly be categorized as psychiatric. It is also a book about a form of human suffering and courage, about some of the routes of interpersonal experience that may lead to such a disaster, and about the use of the human relationship as a source of hope, help, and return from what in times past was referred to as "the living death." Of greater importance, perhaps, is the relevance of these writings to the life styles of all of us, be we schizophrenic or not. Schizophrenia is not easily classified; regardless of the major—and multiple—factors related to its creation and appearance, it reflects a culture, a society, a family, and the life experience of a human being. Within this trouble each of us—if he dares look closely—can find something of himself; it is one of the frightening, even reassuring, caricatures of what we call humanity.

In reading this volume I am reminded of past events in my own personal-psychiatric history, relating them as best I can to the present and to conjectures about the future. Change does take place, but much of it comes blindly and, if noticed at all, it is difficult to evaluate whether it is for the better or the worse. The history of psychiatry can be found in the present, where its existence continues. Our knowledge increases, but the old quarrels, beliefs, doubts, fears, and strange expectations remain with us. It often seems that as we seek to understand behavior and disorder with increasingly scientific and sophisticated methods, we avoid or withdraw from a simpler (yet in subtle ways, more complex) confrontation with ourselves. Even though reduced to the most minute elements, the significances of life and the universe lie beyond our observation or comprehension. Man can study and know himself only through himself, and his view is therefore limited and skewed. Bound by biological restrictions, by culture, and by events (what we term "chance"), he does, nevertheless, have some freedom of choice as to what he is and shall become—that is, man's responsibility for what he is and for what he becomes cannot properly be attributed to ancestry, environment, fate, luck, nature, the gods—or to some mysterious psychiatric disorder. In brief, behaviors defined as "sick" cannot be set aside from the totality of a life; rather, they must be seen as a product of many factors—biologic and social—as well as of personal decision. This is not necessarily a pleasant or welcome concept; nor is it new. Irresistible fate may be less painful than accountability to ourselves and to each other. Even though we are not always masters of our destiny, we need not, in most instances, be passive victims of the circumstances of our existence. To achieve increased freedom of choice, we must attempt to comprehend more fully what we do to one another, observing the good and the bad and learning to differentiate one from the other. What we see may not be pleasant; it may require shedding our illusions and making changes. In this connection, the work of the psychiatrist (and of others) may be both feared and valued. His task is not only to heal, but to reveal the greater healing to come (if it does) through further recognition of interpersonal and social responsibility.

In the past forty-odd years the knowledge of psychiatric matters and human behavior has been enriched particularly by investigations in the following areas:

> interdisciplinary collaborations—the pulling together of efforts in anthropology, sociology, psychology, physiology, biochemistry, and psychiatry;
> the hospital milieu;

the family;
animal behavior (other than human);
the nature of culture;
relationships in individual psychotherapy and larger groups; and
the modification of living through chemical means.

At the present time we find much that we knew in the past. There is disagreement about the adequacy—or appropriateness—of the term "schizophrenia." What is called schizophrenia in one country—or in one hospital—may not be so named in other places. Some professionals insist that the term is a hindrance to observation and thinking, and should therefore be abandoned. There is a wide range of treatments for this difficulty, and the views of various advocates are supported by more or less objective or scientific data. The schizophrenic person (for the time being I shall use the term since it conveys some meaning to me) may be treated in a variety of ways, depending on his social position, economic status, geographic location, personal bias, and professional consultation. He may receive ECT, phenothiazines and other drugs, exposure to a variety of milieus, individual, group, and encounter-psychotherapies, and so on. In any case there will be uncertainty about the nature of the disorder, the prognosis, and the means of judging outcome. Influencing all this are such matters as the social need, the increasing demand for psychiatric care, crowded hospitals, personnel shortage, financial limitations—and the fearsome mythologies of the past. Perhaps there is no one schizophrenia, but a variety of entities or forms of behavior with which we must deal without clear knowledge of causation or of what will come of what we do. Bearing this in mind, we should be cautious in speaking of the "psychotherapy of schizophrenia," for both terms have many meanings. To reduce confusion, it is best, I think, to give an operational description of what we call schizophrenia and psychotherapy.

Treatment can serve the purpose of alleviating distress (of patient and others), furthering understanding, and simply controlling behavior. It is useful to recognize and specify our goals.

A book, through its authors, speaks for itself, and I shall not attempt to speak for it. In this volume we hear about schizophrenia as a way of life, a life style, a mode of existence—that is, the behaviors have meaning in terms of a person's experience (past, present, and future), his family, his society, his culture, his biological endowment. What he does has purpose and is goal-directed, however inadequate and seemingly inappropriate it may be—and, to a large extent, incomprehensible or untranslatable. He is attempting to meet the demands of society and his personal needs through the use of techniques that he has learned in order to deal with anxiety, the complexities of his fellows, the cultural inconsistencies and irrationalities, the vicissitudes of life, and the never-to-be-known mystery of his own existence. From this point of view schizophrenia is not an entity to be considered apart from a man's total life—an idea in keeping with much of modern medical thought in regard to nonpsychiatric difficulties.

We know that the human relationship is a major factor in bringing about behavioral change—for better or worse. But psychotherapy—a process of change and learning—is slow and costly; it is better to learn how to live effectively in the first place than to attempt correction of early misadventures at a later date. Recognizing the needs and demands of society and the restriction of intensive psychotherapy to the few, the procedure should nonetheless be supported and continued. In my view, it is of direct help to some people, and it is a research instrument that should be retained. It is one path to the heart of the matter, for it is designed to reveal more about what our lives are dependent upon: the human relationship. Perhaps we should recurrently remind ourselves that we are both symbolizing and rationalizing creatures, that to a considerable extent we learn to be what we are, and that we create our own mythologies by which we may live or die, without—as far as I know —having any appreciable effect on the universe at large. We can also remind ourselves that we can take a hand in our destiny, modestly aware that to tamper without knowledge and respect for life itself is presumptuous, arrogant, and exceedingly dangerous. From the ways of life that we now call schizophrenia, we may learn something about how we often act to restrict our own development and contribute to our personal and social defeats. Knowledge alone is not enough; it must be combined with wisdom, hope, faith—and a leavening of charity. The authors speak, in their own ways, to this subject.

In summary, the psychotherapist—and all of us—must live with uncertainty, working with determination in a universe that is for him, at least, indeterminate. I close with an excerpt from a poem —"Magic"—by the anthropologist Loren Eiseley:

> This is the root of magic
> and science,
> life's response to
> uncertainties—
> if a thing works
> you try it
> and try once more
> and again
> until
> you are absolutely sure
> it will never work,
> then try it once more.
> That is magic,
> and animals and people
> live or die
> by the uncertainties.*

* Eiseley, Loren, *Notes of an Alchemist,* Charles Scribner's Sons, New York, 1972, p. 67.

PREFACE

For many years now it has been evident to clinicians that the theoretical formulations of Kraepelin and Bleuler on schizophrenia left something to be desired. For the past century, just at the time these conceptions of schizophrenia were being formulated and communicated, culture and its disease and deviant processes were shifting so that both the postulated pathogen for schizophrenia and the healing understanding of it now need to be reconsidered. Even the psychopathology of the delusion and hallucination needs to be revised in face of the wide use of hallucinogenic drugs. The need for the ubiquitous mental hospital may also have passed since the prevalent forms of schizophrenia are now best described by such metaphors as "ambulatory," "petit mal," or "schizophrenics at liberty." *Catatonia, hebephrenia,* and *simplex* have become historical anachronisms, with little relevance to the actual patient who presents himself for treatment.

In going back to pick up the thread of a lost road, it is wise to return to the original and pristine phenomenon itself. It is difficult today to be neutral about schizophrenia—to experience it the way it stands forth in its living and behavioral forms. We tend to impose a framework around it, according to our predilections and training, and this very often obscures what the patient is thinking, feeling, and being. If one becomes able to put the framework aside for a brief moratorium, a surprising thing happens. The person behind the schizophrenia becomes visible and, *mirabile dictu,* his disease does not seem so ultimately pernicious and deteriorative. Indeed, the improved prospects rouse numbers of therapists to try their hand at a psychotherapeutic cure. How, then, has it happened that we have lost the patient while not even finding the disease? This book offers no short cut to curing schizophrenia. Rather, it forces the reader to a reappraisal and reconsideration of what schizophrenia is all about, and it relates the patient more closely to men everywhere, whether sick or not. It even dares to offer new and radical assumptions as to schizophrenia as a possible life style or as a way of being-in-the-world. These possibilities we have found to be inherently related to the patient's condition and to his treatment. Their use permits us to go further in understanding and helping him than any other approach we know of.

Therefore, if this book is at all successful in giving pause to the reader, a pause in which he can soberly reconsider the whole problem of schizophrenia, our work will have been well done.

Arthur Burton

Sacramento, California

SCHIZOPHRENIA
AS A LIFE STYLE

THE DELUSIONAL
SCHIZOPHRENIC MUTATION

Juan J. Lopez-Ibor

I should like to begin with a brief examination of what we denote by the term "schizophrenia." I deliberately say "we denote," for anyone familiar with the history of medicine, however rudimentary his knowledge, is well aware of the immense difficulties presented by the world of disease, especially mental disease.

The history of schizophrenia is basically the history of psychiatry. Let us merely recall that at the end of the nineteenth century a noteworthy effort was made to comprehend the world of disease. A number of diagnostic expressions, some of which dated from earlier times (such as "vesania"), disappeared, while others survived (such as "catatonia").

If problems of medicine are complex, they are all the more so in psychiatry because of the two aspects—somatic and psychological —in which they manifest themselves. Kahlbaum published his book on catatonia in 1874, six years after Griesinger, who looked for cerebral lesions in all mental diseases and for the bridge that linked them to the psychic life. In 1880, Wernicke created the neologism "sejunction" to describe the apparent dehiscence of schizophrenic thought processes. When Morel's term "demence precoce," introduced in 1860, was adopted by Kraepelin himself, its area of appli-

1

cation was further extended. Then came the large group of psychiatrists influenced by the psychologist Wundt, among whom Kraepelin must be included. E. Bleuler is credited with the expression "group of schizophrenias." Hardly had the term "schizophrenia" been introduced when the awareness of its insufficiency, and especially of the great variety of patients included in the designation, led to attempts to further divide the group: paraphrenia, hebephrenia, paranoid dementia, etc. But the designation has persisted, and the various subgroups of the schizophrenic area are now rarely included in the nomenclature.

Arthur Burton has proposed a direct confrontation with the "schizophrenic mode of existence," noting that the problem of such existence is intimately related to that of human existence itself. It is precisely for this reason that those whom we call schizophrenic have always been studied with such intense interest. In schizophrenic existence there is not only a message, but a human metamessage.

In Kraepelin's last work (1920), in which he no longer speaks of diseases but of *modes of becoming diseased,* he stresses the need to know the inner life of man from its early-childhood roots, to integrate the study of primitive man and even of animal psychopathology, in order to get to know better what we can call—and do in fact call—*personal life.* Schizophrenics are all around us in the clinics, or we see them in the street, as people who are not interesting now but perhaps may have once been. When we study them, however, we discover the peculiar authenticity of their mode of existing.

The designation "schizophrenia" or "group of schizophrenias" achieved a remarkable degree of success. In the view of the psychiatrists of the time, having found a "nosological entity" that was clinically well defined, the next step was the study of its etiology, its clinical forms, and its treatment. As a result, the mass of accumulated data has been extraordinary, and it is advisable that we reflect on the significance of these advances.

At the outset, the disease was approached from the point of view of biology and psychology. E. Bleuler's example, cited in 1911, is indeed memorable: in a case of osteomalacia, the morbid process is determined by the chemical and physical alterations, and even by the decalcification of the bone. Thus weakened, a bone can suffer a fracture, which in this case will not be the immediate primary sequel of the morbid process, but a secondary one. Hence the necessity of distinguishing between fundamental and accessory symptoms. Among the *fundamental* symptoms, E. Bleuler includes the disorder of thought associations, which are not only split but condensed or merged; on other occasions they displace the meaning of one idea onto another, or the patient suffers from interceptions or eruptions of thinking, or from inhibition of the latter. Affectivity is altered in the form of affective ambivalence; at times, intellectual and volitional ambivalence—and, on other occasions, autism—appears. Among the *accessory* symptoms, Bleuler includes hallucinations, delusional ideas, certain alterations in memory, and catatonic symptoms (stereotypy, impulsive acts, etc.).

Bleuler laid great stress on *autism*. Every person, in his opinion, has the need to compensate with his imagination that which reality denies to him; and only by giving himself over to autism can he fulfill that need. Autism is not an armor that immobilizes the mind of the schizophrenic; rather, it is a kind of defensive shield to be utilized on occasion, as if one were a gladiator. Such an occasion arises when the patient finds it impossible to maintain a firm and solid attitude with regard to himself, which is what the "I" needs to establish with itself, and with the external world if it is to maintain its identity. As Manfred Bleuler aptly recalls, such interpretation has been adopted by many collaborators of E. Bleuler—Eugen Minkowski, Ludwig Binswanger, Jacob Wyrsch, and Christian Müller in Europe, and a considerable number of psychiatrists in the U.S.A., such as Silvano Arieti, Redlich, and many others. The major interest here lies in its opening up a variety of psychotherapeutic approaches, for autism masks many sentiments and attitudes, such as aggressiveness against certain people or against the world, as well as anxiety, nostalgic presentiments of still a different existence, etc. In many cases it seems as if autism is not an armor, as I have observed above, but a mask that permits the schizophrenic to conceal a strange, delusional world—sometimes destructive and, at times, creative and poetic. Behind this mask the schizophrenic can feel omnipotent or helpless, as Burton says. Taking refuge behind it, he can fear his own destruction or that of those who love him. M. Bleuler calls attention to the glance of the schizophrenic, who at times seems to say, "Please accept me as I am," as though asking for protection.

Freud said that he was not interested in the facts observed but in what was beneath the facts—that is to say, in their interpretation. As Kant expressed it, what is important is not the phenomenon but the *noumemon*.* The truth is that the series of psychological alterations manifesting themselves in the state we call *schizophrenia* is so variable, and constitutes such an inextricable magma, that it is difficult to obtain greater clarity in the description of the *intimate structure* of the internal events of the patient. On the other hand, there is no greater enemy of clarity than success. Bleuler, who eagerly sought to clarify the problem of schizophrenia, did not suspect what would happen subsequently.

In November 1970, the World Association of Psychiatry organized a "Symposium on Uses and Abuses of Psychiatry" in London. Most of the participants were psychiatrists, but the organizers wisely invited writers and intellectuals to attend. One of these was Arthur Koestler, whose remarks underscored what we all know: the tremendous ambiguity of the word "schizophrenia." These ambiguities may occur more frequently in the humanities than in the natural sciences; but what is decisive is that when we establish a diagnosis of schizophrenia, we are speaking of a human being. Koestler regretted the varying diagnoses for any single patient, depending on whether he was seen in Europe or in the U.S.A. The disparities do not signify diagnostic errors, but different conceptions. The World Health Organization has attempted various experiments to unify the criteria, but has not yet found it possible to do so. Neither hereditary and constitutional studies nor biochemical studies have succeeded in clarifying the question. Despite all the divergent criteria, the use of the diagnosis of schizophrenia is helpful if some essential factors are taken into account.

The scope of the word "schizophrenia" has changed with time. At the outset, in the works of Kraepelin and others, the ideal of psy-

---

* *Noumemon,* a term utilized by Plato to designate that which is known by the spirit (*nous*) and not by the senses.

chiatry consisted in attaining something analogous to the discoveries relating to general paralysis. The schizophrenics we saw in the clinic two or more decades ago were serious cases; hebephrenia, catatonia, and the paranoid forms of schizophrenia constituted three seemingly well-defined types. By comparison with the oscillations and remissions of manic-depressive psychosis, they formed a distinctive group. With time, the situation changed—on the one hand, due to the progress made in helping psychiatric therapeutics and, on the other hand, due to the deeper psychological study of the patient. I recall my first visit to a psychiatric clinic when I was still studying medicine. There, in a country where psychiatry had the reputation of having made advances, I was able to see a number of catatonic patients. Today, several years elapse without my seeing any such patients.

Now the panorama is quite distinct. Schizophrenics are no longer the most numerous patients in a modern psychiatric hospital. They are seen in the outpatient department and are treated the same way as most other patients. And the number of those whom I would call "schizophrenics at liberty" is astonishing. Schizophrenic acute outbreaks pass. I have seen such outbreaks that were not renewed after fifteen or twenty years. I have seen young men resume and complete their university studies after a schizophrenic episode. The army of "schizophrenics at liberty" grows daily; and the increase began even before the introduction of new neuroleptic therapies.

The increase is not due to a change in diagnostic limits, nor to indiscriminate use of the word "schizophrenia," but to a change in the manifestations of the disease itself and in the relationship with patients. Have we not seen the change in the symptomatology of neurosis (or, if you prefer, of hysteria) between the last two world wars? To speak of a "madman" once caused fear. We were faced with the "hideous." Today we encounter different manifestations. Take the case of two young women, aged eighteen and sixteen, whose exploits are being described in the French press as I write these lines. They bought two knives and hitchhiked until they managed to get a ride. On the pretext that something had fallen, they asked the driver to stop and pick it up. Taking advantage of his position as he bent down, they stabbed him in the back. They had attempted to do this to two other men. The first driver seemed suspicious of them, and they desisted; the second one was "trop gentil"; the third man became the victim. The sixteen-year-old fled, but the older girl stood petrified throughout the incident, trying to find a motive for her behavior. Neither girl suffered from any mental disturbance.

The difference, then, is quite evident. The notion of what we call schizophrenia has totally changed.* As I see it, schizophrenia has become more refined in its manifestations, and there has become a more limited aspect of that which really constitutes the *schizophrenic*.

The question I am trying to raise is: What is the essence of that which we can call the *schizophrenic existence?*

Man is not a pure biological being. This is one of the great errors of modern medicine, although on many occasions a physician, without doing serious harm, may act as though this were the case. Another great error, in the inverse sense, is that of certain schools of psychology and psychotherapy which ignore the biological.

An important aspect of a more comprehensive definition of man is the fact that he is a *historic* being. While it may seem irrelevant to insist on this, it is not so pointless when it is not only a question of his external history but of his internal one as well.

Anthropologists discuss the origin of man at great length. According to Claude Lévi-Strauss, the transition between the world of nature and the world of culture is characterized by the prohibition of the rule of incest; that is to say, not of incest in itself, but of the appearance of a *rule* that is no longer a biological mechanism but a cultural manifestation. The Pharaohs did not understand incest as we do today; for them, union was possible only with a first-born sister, not with others, for it signified the rule of conserving the royal

---

* Let us leave aside the problem of drug addicts. On one occasion a psychiatrist in another country was accompanying a drug addict to have him admitted to a clinic. As the young addict was leaving the aircraft, he tried to escape, without success. The psychiatrist remarked, "How mistaken I was in his diagnosis! He is certainly a schizophrenic." Such improper use of psychiatric terms is widespread. The drug addict in question did something that was not clinically anomalous; he wanted to avoid being taken involuntarily to a clinic to be treated.

charisma. However, since some anthropologists dispute the premise of Lévi-Strauss, let us choose another principle, and one that is no less important: *language.* It is not enough, in speaking of human language, to refer to the problem of *communication*—for example, among bees. It is language itself, which is invented in the course of human development, whose comprehension we find only when we penetrate its great vectors of communication: the past, the present, and the future. Other living beings, persons and things, disease, and life and death are matters about which we can obtain information through language. To understand this language we need not cease to be mute. Physical defects pose some difficulties, but to conquer —or not to lose—in this struggle with difficulties amounts to constituting oneself as a person. Only thus do we discover that we live in a *personal world* with its own horizons, which will afford each person the potential of transforming life into experiences, possibilities into realities, desires into renunciations or acceptances, etc.

In connection with the schizophrenic existence, there is an even more interesting question. How is what we generally denote as "the world" constituted? Precisely by means of the "historicity" of life. It is not a question of providing life with furnishings, as if it were a house, but of the internal elaboration of events, permitting each person to achieve his own *personal* life. Man lives in a world of *meanings,* which is not the same as a world of things that lack sense. Thus, to the degree that our life becomes organized, so, too, does that network of meanings which we call one's own world. Language aids in establishing this personal order, yet it is not everything—it is the gaze, the object one stumbles upon, the falling star that passes silently when we observe the firmament. Some of these phenomena and events will be displaced to a periphery from which they will never (or possibly rarely) emerge; others will remain; and still others will *change in meaning.* It is in the specific nature of this change in meaning that we find the possibility of the *schizophrenic existence,* for this change offers something uniquely different from the changes in normal daily life.

A great poet, a friend of mine, manifested his first schizophrenic symptom when he observed people gathering in the square after they left work. He had seen this often, but on this particular occasion the gathering was transformed into an apocalyptic sign on the basis of which he developed a severe schizophrenic delusion. Another patient, a woman, after remaining silent for several days, abandoning her work, and doing without sleep or food, said that on the first day, on returning home, she had seen a number on the door of a shop (corresponding to the numbering of the street). There were several figures, but only the number "7" attracted her attention, because that 7 *"was or signified"* the serpent—the sin which had made her fall sexually. From that moment on, her sad and anxious behavior of the previous weeks was illuminated. Even though she told her mother what had happened—she had had an amorous adventure—it failed to tranquilize her about the anomalous meaning of that number 7; instead, there now appeared, without the initial anxiety, a proliferation of multiple and diverse meanings that lasted several weeks.

Another case concerned a boy who heard an unpleasant word while walking along the street. When questioned, he was not sure that the word was "pansy," or if the word was expressed by the look that a stranger had directed toward him. A few days later he insisted that the stranger had looked at him and insulted him, and that he had told this to other people. Now, everybody thinks that he is a "homosexual." Had he become homosexual? Was it possible? The conversation at various interviews was concerned with this subject. Two days later he returned to say: *Yes, he had become homosexual.* This brief chain terminated in a suicide attempt, which motivated the intervention of the psychiatrist. The world had changed in design for the patient. Zutt speaks of the physiognomic-esthetic quality with which the world expresses itself, apart from being an object of knowledge. Perhaps for us it would be sufficient to speak of the *physiognomy* with which we see the world. In that of the schizophrenic there appear one or more *new* meanings which infiltrate and substitute various habitual meanings, precisely because of their phenomenologically different quality.

These are some examples. The variety of changes in experiences are great. But can a poet or a painter offer us an analogous change in such experiences? Analogous, yes, but in essence different if it occurs in the field of normality. For this reason, it is necessary to isolate the "lived-through" experiences, which K. Schneider has called *primary* symptoms of schizophrenia. By *primary,* we do not mean that they are genetically primary; rather, they are *characteristic* or *pathognomonic,* as referred to in classical medicine. The *secondary* symptoms are, in principle, less reliable in defining a patient as schizophrenic. In order to establish the diagnosis, the presence of the primary symptoms is not absolutely necessary. The *primary symptoms* of schizophrenia are:

1. Thought, hearing, or echoing—*"écho de la pensée."*
2. Thought in the form of dialogue (hearing voices in the form of a dialogue between the patient and people or strange beings).
3. Hearing comments on one's own actions, even the most habitual or commonplace.
4. "Lived-through" experiences of corporal influence.
5. Interference with thought (theft of thought and other analogous influences).
6. Thought diffused among other people.
7. Delusional perception.
8. All the other experiences pertaining to the emotional or volitional life that have the character of being imposed.

As I have already pointed out, there are many other symptoms, such as impulsive acts, catatonias, autism, verbigerations, etc., which make it possible to establish the diagnosis; but *the presence of a single one of the primary symptoms suffices.* These symptoms are observed, above all, in the first phase of the disease, or when it undergoes a period of reactivation. On the other hand, the secondary symptoms correspond to more stabilized pictures.

However, if any one of the previously mentioned symptoms is analyzed, its psychological impurity can be observed. In other words, when we *think,* our thought does not acquire the quality of being converted into *sound,* it is not diffused as through a loudspeaker, and we do not see what appears on the television screen as being directed at us, etc. That is to say, the psychological functions in the schizophrenic have become *contaminated* with something that really pertains to the province of another psychological func-

tion, and hence acquire a *new and distinct meaning*. Through this
mutation, the patient penetrates, totally or partially, into a *metaphorical world* whose existence had never been revealed to him in
this manner. It is as though he felt himself invaded by a magical or
numinous atmosphere.

During periods when a schizophrenic outbreak is beginning, the
patient may attain the simultaneous coexistence of the two existential planes, the delusional and the normal, which is what should
really be called schizophrenia. The variety in the course of the disease, the intensity and persistence of the picture, the enormous fragility of many of its contents—all have significance in chronic cases
to the extent that there is no realization of this simultaneous living
in two worlds. At times, the patient may totally deliver himself over
to one of them: *the personality of each patient is thus revealed*—
above all, his own *internal history,* which does not consist of what a
person does every day or on a given day, but of the "peculiar" trace
that it leaves behind.

The importance of the above symptoms is not *prognostic,* but it
facilitates the diagnosis. Many acute schizophrenic outbreaks cease
in a few days, sometimes spontaneously, and even more rapidly
when submitted to therapy. This is precisely one of the most crucial
moments: the person must not lose contact with his own world before the intromission of this *physiognomic change* in all or part of
it. At the same time, while neuroleptics are of aid, *existential psychotherapy* is essential.

Let us now examine in detail some of the ideas in the literature
about delusions. Those who doubt the importance of phenomenological psychology should examine the data obtained by an analysis
of the delusional experience. When the classical clinicians tried to
find a definition of the delusional idea, they committed a veritable
petitio principii, as can now be seen.

> "A delusional idea is an error morbidly engendered, and at the
> same time incorrigible." (Rümke)
> "A delusional idea is a representation morbidly falsified and
> incorrigible." (Hoch)
> "A delusional idea is an error arising from the feeling of mean-

ing that is morbidly altered; it is incorrigible, because it is 'lived through' as being immovably certain." (Bleuler)

"A delusional idea is a morbidly falsified representation." (Kraepelin, 1883)

"Delusional ideas are errors engendered in a morbid manner, which are not accessible to justification by motivated fundaments." (Kraepelin-Lange, 1927)

As may be seen, in all these definitions the word "morbid" intervenes. The error is a delusional error when it is engendered morbidly; but that is *precisely* what we must verify: that such an error or such an idea, even though not erroneous, *has a morbid origin*. Non-phenomenological psychopathology appeals, in such cases, to the characteristics of the content to demonstrate the morbidity of the error. Jaspers summarized these characteristics in the following three points: (1) the extraordinary conviction with which they are maintained, and their extraordinary subjective certitude; (2) the impenetrability to experience and to logical refutation; and (3) the unlikelihood of the content.

But these three characteristics are not always sufficient to define a delusional idea, although on many occasions they may be. There are delusional ideas which are credible. On many occasions the patient does not show himself so absolutely impenetrable to refutation. We frequently say to a schizophrenic, when in his initial phase he tells us that people on the street look at him in a special way, or they make signs to him when entering a cafe, "But how can you believe you are so important that everybody is concerned with you?" And some patients reply, perplexedly, "Yes, it really can't be so, but something strange must be happening." Here we encounter the failure of that extraordinary conviction and that absolute criterion of subjective certainty mentioned above.

In the search for characterization of this morbid origin of delusional ideas, the phenomenological school distinguishes between *primary and secondary delusional ideas*. The secondary ideas derive from a "lived-through" experience that precedes them—for example, the delusional idea of ruin of the melancholic, which is engendered by a sad mood. We could speak of *explicable and inexplicable* delusional ideas. That a melancholic should believe himself to be ruined is an explicable delusional idea; but it is really inexplicable when someone begins to believe that all those who put their handkerchiefs to their noses are homosexuals.

As a result of the phenomenological analysis of different forms of delusion, the following are distinguished: (1) delusional perception; (2) delusional happening; and (3) delusional reaction (delusional "lived-through" reaction).

Delusional perception is spoken of when a real perception is given an abnormal meaning, without the presence of a rational or emotive comprehensible motive. The meaning, as a general rule (with some exceptions), is directed to the "I"—it has the character of self-reference.

Delusional perception must be differentiated from the self-reference that has a comprehensible motive. In this case, it is based not so much on false interpretations as on determined moods, such as anxiety, distrust, suspicion, etc. An example of this is the boy who fears that his mother, merely by looking at him, will discover that he has masturbated. Jaspers called this group "deliroid ideas" or, to put it more simply, "deliroid reaction." The delusional idea is fully integrated into the existing mood, and for this reason it is comprehensible.

What is the basis of the most essential and peremptory characteristics of delusional perception? Gruhle says that it is a question of "establishing a relationship without a motive." A patient of ours saw a passenger sneeze in a bus. The patient immediately believed that the sneeze meant he was a homosexual. It is precisely in this reference to oneself that the essential feature is based. In 1911, Loewy was already speaking of the *"Rufcharakter"*—the "character of calling" or the "allusive" nature of such delusional ideas—and Wernicke pointed out the "transitiveness" of these ideas. It is only *this reference to the "I"* that is abnormal, and Specht, who recognized the role of affectivity in delusional ideas, stated that such ideas do not exist if the "I" is not situated *in the center of them.* The unusual irruption of this reference to the "I," surprising the patient himself, is what betrays the morbid and irreducible character of the delusional idea. It is thus understandable that a *delusional perception* ("the delusion is already perceived") has been spoken of to express this phenomenon of reference to oneself or this feeling oneself alluded to without any motive.

As to the part of the delusion that does not enter into the delusional perception, it is possible to speak of a "delusional happening"; included in this designation are such happenings as being called to a political or religious mission, or being possessed by a special quality, or being persecuted or loved. We could more fittingly speak of a "delusional inspiration." What distinguishes the delusional perception from the delusional inspiration is precisely the fact that in one instance one becomes integrated with the perception, but not in the other.

Delusional perception is bimembral when it is submitted to structural analysis. The first member extends from the subject who perceives to the object perceived, including the common significations perceived by all. The second member goes from the object perceived (with its normal significations) to the anomalous signification. For example, a person perceives a dog lifting its leg; for the delusional subject, this lifting of the leg, perceived in the same way as other people perceive it, signifies *something special*. The fundamental structure of the delusional idea is precisely its *bipolar* nature. *The underivability, the incomprehensibility, of this second pole is decisive.* In this respect it is distinguished from normal symbolic thinking. It could be said that in the symbolic experiences of the nonpsychotic life there exists—behind the perception, with its normal significance—a second member, made up of the symbolic "lived-through" experience. This second member is comprehensible, individually or collectively, and such interpretations pertain for us to the first member. When a young person plucks the first spring violet and sees in this the sign of love, this love can be understood in the light of his mood. When a four-leaf clover signifies "happiness" to its finder, the interpretation is rationally comprehensible because of its collective determination. When a man changes his course because a black cat has just crossed his path, its sinister meaning continues to be a comprehensible interpretation of a perception for it is based on a collective judgment. It is precisely behind these comprehensible interpretations that there commences, "without motive," the second characteristic pole in delusional perception. As for the rest, the manner of being affected in the delusional perception, the second pole—namely, *the attributed significance*—is different from normal perception. It appears to be a "numinous" experience of a special class.

The delusional happening or inspiration is unimembral; consequently, it lacks the specific structure of the delusional perception and has less validity for diagnosis. A delusional perception suffices to reveal the presence of a schizophrenia, whereas delusional inspiration causes one to think of it. But the diagnosis must be assured by the presence of other symptoms or by general consideration of the clinical course, etc. At times, delusional inspirations are not differentiated from the happenings of normal life—for example, an overvalued preoccupation or a superstitious belief. A delusional happening or inspiration can be possible and still be morbid—for example, being loved by a woman neighbor. On the other hand, there are grotesque happenings that are not delusional.

In normal perception there is first a sensorial component, followed by a structural organization; this constitutes the true perceptive act. While this structure contains various ingredients, the essential element is the *significance attributed to the object perceived.* Its significance derives from previous experience, and the subject introduces this significant aspect into the perceptive act. Without this there would be no authentic perception, but a complex of sensorial points—*there would be sensations, but not things.* This significance can be habitual or symbolic. The normal man attributes symbolic meanings to his perception; hence the character of this symbolism is outside of the delusional idea. Some symbols are linked by a particular experimental or rational connection (e.g., the use of the flag as the symbol of a country); others are linked by less obvious analogies (e.g., metaphors in poetry). When a poet creates a new metaphor, it also has a special symbolic significance for him, one that the rest of us can understand and accept, or reject as incomprehensible; yet we never describe it as a delusional idea, however strange and improbable it may be.

To say that delusional perception is characterized by its symbolic relationships is evidently insufficient. The sane person also has his symbolic interpretations. Nietzsche said that language is a highway of metaphors. In this connection, Gruhle recalls Bachoffen's book, *Gräbersymbolik der Alten*. The sane man is capable of deciphering the symbolic interpretations, basing himself on his knowledge or on analogies.

On occasion, it is difficult to interpret by analogy, or on the basis of one's own knowledge, some images in modern poetry. Rather, it is necessary, as I see it—and this is the goal of the poet—to make it possible for an experience to be relived in a new way.

All poetic expression is replete with allusions. And the notion that all reality can be expressed by means of habitual language is incorrect. Is language capable of expressing what is felt in the plenitude of sexual or amorous possession? When, in place of everyday reality, we find ourselves, like the patient, confronting the new reality of a psychotic world, the insufficiency of language is still more evident. In the first phase of indetermination there is always an obscure perception, like a message from a new and different world. When the message seems indecipherable, the patient feels *a disturbing strangeness;* but when he succeeds in glimpsing some sense in it, he begins to experience tranquility.

In addition, what clearly characterizes delusional perception is that *the patient experiences this significance as being imposed.* When the poet discovers a new metaphor, he experiences a certain *feeling of activity.* In ordinary perception, there is always an activity of the person that is turned toward the world, on the basis of which the person derives a certain deep and obscure impression. If we do not submit to any self-analysis, we live in the erroneous belief that perception is a purely passive process. In reality, the totality of psychic life is characterized by activeness, though there are diverse degrees of activity, such as those that mediate between the voluntary actions of moving the arm and the passive perception of the ray of sunlight that penetrates the room.

In delusional perception, the subject has the impression that that significance which basically arises from himself (from where else, if it does not?) *is strangely imposed upon him.* Thus, the primary delusional idea offers us the same psychological structure as other behavior in the life of the schizophrenic, and these, taken as a whole, can be interpreted as *disturbances of the activity of the "I."*

The existence of a mood is the precursor of a delusional perception, and we should suspect that it always exists. According to Guiraud, "Mais la caractéristique du malaise thymique prédélirante est un cachet d'étrangeté inquiétante, *ne semblant pas provenir de l'activité somatique ou psychique individuelle.*"

It is to this vague and undefined period, revealed only by a special state of mood, that Clerambault refers when he says that at the moment when the delusion appears the psychosis is already longstanding. The delusion is merely a superstructure.

When the delusional mood precedes the idea, the patient notes something rare and strange surrounding him. He cannot define what it is, even if he makes an effort to avoid it, since the delusional mood is so tormenting in the intimate zone of the patient's life that when he succeeds in filling it with meaning, he experiences a certain relief. This fact means that that which characterizes delusional perception does not only consist in merely conceding a determined sense to the perception. The distinctive note is necessarily found in the vague and diffuse perception that something strange is happening around him. Naturally, in the majority of cases, all these fragments, which I am endeavoring to interpret here as images of a film, proceed more rapidly, and then suddenly the patient, seeing an object or a person, attributes a given symbolic significance to the circumstance.

The delusional mood expresses the singular and abnormal state perceived by schizophrenics in their inner life. It is not only a question of the perplexity one observes in their faces. It is something else—the sensation of the arcane, the strange, the singular. This mixture of becoming aware of a thing together with a strong affective impregnation is known to normal psychology. Goethe, for example, refers to an affective knowing, which *colors reality with something spectral*—i.e., the experience invades, so to speak, more than one sector of the psychic life. In the primary delusional experience of the schizophrenic, this invasion takes place so suddenly that it surprises the patient. The irruption is not a pure intellectual assault, but it disturbs his state.

Delusional mood and ideas are pieces, fragments, of the same psychic experience. For us, the external observers, one or the other attracts our attention more, *but it is not possible to establish an irreducible hiatus between them.*

We believe that this feature of feeling surprised by the experience is fundamental. Whether the patient feels himself alluded to, or if the "omens" are manifested to him as communicating their portents to him, he has the impression of being a passive subject in this experience. The delusional idea *is revealed* to the patient. I propose designating this as *delusional revelation* because it seems to expound, in a more precise manner, exactly what happens in the patient than does *delusional perception.*

Rather than conceding too much value to the presence of the delusional mood in the genesis of delusional ideas, one must consider disparities that can exist between the state of the mood and the very nature of the delusional perception. Precisely because of its indetermination, it is said, the mood of the schizophrenic cannot determine the content of the delusional perception. It is buried in him, but is not derived from him. Nor does it even coincide with the tone of the mood. A delusional mood can be ominous, and the delusional perception can expand with happiness.

How can we recognize the existence of a mood? In normal life, a mood is revealed in words. A person says that he is happy, sad, anxious, euphoric, etc. Sometimes we can infer a mood from its expression. This also happens with schizophrenics. What is known as *"Praecoxgefühl"* (Rümke)—what we call the "odor of schizophrenia" (in the jargon of the clinic, "It smells to me like a schizophrenic," or "I have the presentiment that we are dealing with a schizophrenic")—is based, in part, on our impression of the patient's gestures, attitudes, and behavior.

But the articulated expression of a mood may not prove to be so easy. Detailed analysis of many of my patients suffering from anxiety indicates how frequently they are incapable of saying that they are suffering from anxiety. Indeed, when asked directly, they deny it. On the other hand, when they speak to us, their voices thicken as they report that when they see a murder in a film or come close to a mental patient, they experience a special sensation which is more acute than a habitual mood. This experience, correctly interpreted, signifies a fear of the possibility of becoming a criminal, of going mad, etc.; it represents pure anxiety, since, as I have shown in other works, the *anxiety of the neurotic is the fear of the possibility of losing control of his "I."* The mood of the schizophrenic is apparently equal to the mood of the anxiety-ridden neurotic, but the internal structure is distinct. In neurotic anxiety, everything *can happen;* in schizophrenic anxiety, something strange, enigmatic, and uninterpretable *is already happening.*

Thus, the problem is found in the degree and variety of the moods. When a mood is clearly perceptible for the subject, it has a well-defined character. We speak of a sad, a happy, an exalted mood. However, the delusional mood never presents itself with a clarity that can be experienced by the patient himself. The sad person defines himself as sad, but the delusional person does not define his interior state as delusional. At most, he employs the vague expression that something is happening but he cannot define it. At a given moment this vagueness is transformed into concrete perception—"they are looking at me"—and the world becomes full of meanings. But it is precisely in these degrees that there exists the possibility of recognizing the delusional perception or revelation.

In existential philosophy, the starting point is analysis of the moods (Heidegger, Bollnow). The anxiety that serves as a point of departure for existential analysis is not a "lived-through" experience, but a vital structure. By remaining on the psychological plane, we could establish the same distinction between the "lived-through" experience and its structure, which cannot be "lived-through." Some who suffer from anxiety, when questioned, do not admit that they are anxious, as we have said earlier. However, the presence of the mood is revealed in another manner: the patient is afraid that he is going mad, or that something rare or strange will happen to him. He reveals, with other words, the same mood.

In the delusion, it appears as an *inversion of the intentional ar-*

row. Our psychic acts have an intentional character, which is seen to be recognized from outside; but there also exists in us a diffuse awareness that the intentions reside *in* us and not outside. In the delusional patient, the reverse happens; the intentions are found outside, in external beings. For this reason, the world is filled with magical meanings, which are not precisely threatening; they are simply surprising.

In the delusional mood it is not the *possibility, but the presence —almost like reality—*of something. And this something is *loaded with intention with respect to the delusional subject.* He feels himself an instrument in the magic hands of his circumstance. The frequency with which these patients read something into the glances of other people can thus be explained. The change in the intentional direction is evident. The new meanings revealed do not necessarily have to be impregnated with a threatening coloration. At times, when there is an obscure presentiment that something is happening, and the presentiment is then confirmed in a look, a gesture, or a sign, the patient is filled with happiness. At other times, the patient feels that he has been chosen so that such a message may be revealed to him. As a result, the mood may not be threatening and hostile, as seems to be the case whenever delusional mood is spoken of.

Thus, the structure of the delusional idea reveals the existence of a qualitative abnormality in the perceptive act, which is characterized by the subject feeling that the obscure, "lived-through" experience of his active relation with the world (a centripetal movement) has been replaced by a relationship of anomalous passivity (a centrifugal movement). For this reason, the content of the act takes strange and unaccustomed forms. And for this reason, too, the delusional idea is anomalous because of its own content. The old definitions of tne delusional idea, which attributed to it the character of a fixed error—one that is improbable, alogical, etc.—allude to the characteristics of the content and *are not valid*. What is defined should not enter into the definition.

By these paths, we arrive at the same point. The psychic life feels itself *subjugated by something.* It has lost its liberty, and the something that subjugates it is the disturbed matter. There is no doubt that this perturbation is definitively established in the relations of the subject with the world and, consequently, of the being-in-the-world. It follows that patients suffering from delusion can be susceptible to an existential-analytic interpretation, apart from the pure phenomenological analysis.

In order to emphasize the clinical value of these analyses, it is sufficient to state two facts:

1. As I have already said, when in a clinical picture we find ourselves with a primary delusional idea, we can be certain that it is almost always a question of a schizophrenia or, if not, of an alcoholic hallucination or an epileptic psychosis. In a certain sense, these latter disturbances become similar to symptomatic psychosis. Thus, the delusional idea has an extraordinary value.

2. Experience shows that the *primary delusional ideas almost never appear alone in the clinical picture.* This finding has the following explanation: since a disturbance of the activity of the "I" is inherent in such ideas, it is logical to think that these can manifest themselves in other sectors of the psychic life—for example, in the hallucinations of impulses, etc.

As we have just seen, in the schizophrenic the new meaning appears suddenly, without its affective infrastructure becoming clear to us. In this connection, we are confronted by a crucial question. Will it not be the case that both all the primary symptoms and the secondary symptoms are due to an *existential mutation of the personality?* Researchers have always sought the common background, the fundamental mood, as the essential nucleus of the schizophrenic. On most occasions, he appears anxiety-ridden; but when we employ such a term, we must bear in mind that his anxiety is not like that of the depressive or of the neurotic. Precisely because of the occurrence of so grave a phenomenon as a mutation, there can coexist psychological facts of a different or varied sense. That is to say, the structure of the normal person is broken, and *the physiognomy of the world in which he lives changes.* The process can continue, and the personality then proceeds to become decomposed and disintegrated. Or it can cicatrize, so to speak, before invading the whole of it. This cicatrization is a partial remission.

The schizophrenic ends by elaborating for himself another existential mode of his own, one of whose characteristics, in many intermediate phases, is that of versatility. We have already said that the schizophrenic does not "hear voices" as an isolated symptom, like auditive hallucinations, but that *people speak to him,* that one or several persons direct themselves to him. It is strange how difficult it is to obtain a response from the patient to the very simple request that he identify the person or persons who speak to him. At times, as an indirect reply, he says that they alluded to him or said something on the radio or during a television program. It is not the hearing of words as dialogue, or the experiencing of hallucinations or kinesthetic sensations in some part of the body (more frequently, in the genital parts), but the fact that all the psychic facts correspond to that new world which is being structured. This is what comprises the *world of the schizophrenic.*

One of my patients comes to see me every four to five years, when his symptoms increase, because he feels the immediate danger that "they" are going to poison him. "They" have a new poison that is more potent than the previous one. He knows that "they" will put it in his food or in his drink. He does not know who "they" are or what they propose. In spite of such delusional threats, he goes to work every day and does his job (in an office of a labor organization) without anyone, except his sister with whom he lives, ever hearing him speak of the delusion. Aside from these delusional recurrences, there are long periods—even years—during which all these strange experiences diminish and do not harass him. His life has changed since the first outbreak: he has separated himself from friends and fellow workers, he takes a walk after work, and he returns home and entertains himself with television—unless he perceives an allusion on the screen that makes him go to his room at once. He has already spent twenty years in this personal and empty world that he has created as an enclave. On other occasions, when more acute phases are involved, with continuous delusional references, he gives up going outside. During some very acute outbreaks, the content of his delusion changes by taking an apocalyptic form (the world comes to an end). Acute outbreaks, even in young people, and according to present-day experience, can in many cases follow their course without leaving any residue. I have seen many such cases which have become cured or remitted. After a lapse of ten, fifteen, or more years, these patients return. They are married and have children, and they now seek consultation not because of illness but because, after marrying without medical advice and having a child, the husband told his wife about his illness and she wanted the doctor to see them, *just in case.*

Some years ago two types were distinguished in the process-formation of schizophrenia: (1) "paranoia," i.e., the delusional form, and (2) "paraphrenia." The two types were broken down into special forms up to the point where each was described as a special disease. Clinical experience has clearly demonstrated that it is a question of evolutive forms of schizophrenia.

What are known as paraphrenic forms are schizophrenias of long duration, but mitigated in their symptomatology and more or less organized in their residual delusions. Hence the psychopathological interest in these manifestations, since in these cases it is seen that the delusion is not simply a fable of a destructured mind—which happens at times—but the elaboration of primordial images analogous to the archaic images of primitive man. It is not a question of historically elaborated mythical forms, but of forms that are mythical in their most primitive purity. Sarro speaks of mythologems. It is a fact that, thanks to therapeutic advances, patients of this group are now hardly seen, and that, sometimes spontaneously and other times thanks to psychotherapeutic action or to the neuroleptics, they live with the images of normal life. At times, primitive images of the origin or the end of the world were disturbing at their beginning, but later they remain in the mind like the old chromolithographs of childhood without any evocative potentiality.

All too often the problem of schizophrenia is posed as though it were a dilemma. In line with the classic history of the disease until Bleuler's time, many psychiatrists have been inclined to consider it an exclusively somatic disease. Despite all the efforts that have been made, it has not been possible to discover an anatomopathological lesion or a biochemical alteration, and attention has been concentrated on a possible inherited basis for it. Again, although

Freud was very cautious with regard to the affirmation of its psychic origin, publication of the Schreber case has stimulated the appearance of analogous cases, which now bypass any commentary on the differences between paranoia as a psychic development and schizophrenia as a disease.

The present approach, however, differs from that of many years ago, and its fundamental principle consists, as I see it, in avoiding all separation and in seeking an anthropological point of view—not only in psychiatric diseases but also in those which are corporal or somatic. To verify the importance of the latter, it is sufficient for us to think of the difference that really exists between the body and corporality (the animated body).

Needless to say, considerable advances are continually being achieved in many aspects of somatic medicine; but reality shows that along with such progress the psychologization of medicine becomes more evident. On the other hand, aid to the mentally ill improves every day. It would be a grave error to forget the progress achieved in the organization of this aid, as well as the large number of mental patients who are treated without being hospitalized. In the Clinical Hospital at the University of Madrid, 40 percent of the outpatients come for psychiatric services usually given to in-patients. In addition, therapeutics by means of neuroleptics, thymoleptics, etc., contribute to this greater efficacy of present-day psychiatry. The fact is so evident that it is unnecessary to insist on its demonstration.

For this reason, even for those who accept the fundamental fact that there is a somatic background in the genesis of schizophrenia, it should not be forgotten that the schizophrenic, like any other somatic patient, requires an adequate psychotherapy—of course, in addition to modifications in the new types of psychiatric aid that are becoming more widespread.

Many psychotherapies have arisen in the field of schizophrenia. Their proliferation, especially in the United States, makes the problem more difficult. Present-day texts on psychiatry concern themselves especially with problems of therapeutic aid and, increasingly, with drug-based therapeutics.

Many psychotherapeutic experiments have not had the success

they promised. In my opinion, the dramatic methods, such as those of Rosen and Sechehaye, have had a somewhat transient success. Hoch passed severe judgment on the results obtained by Rosen, and in many European clinics there is still a conviction that Sechehaye's famous patient, Renee, was not a schizophrenic.

On the other hand, some conventional psychotherapeutic methods, and others that are less conventional, are considered dangerous to many schizophrenic patients. Many experienced psychotherapists hold that the interpretation of dreams should not be attempted in the acute phase of the psychosis. Matussek emphasizes this point, as well as the observation that the use of any form of mental associations in the acute schizophrenic should be rejected as dangerous.

Nevertheless, Pohlen, Siirala, Benedetti, Arieti, and others stress the possibility of a more or less classically psychoanalytic approach in schizophrenia. Pohlen says that in schizophrenia the determining motive is homosexuality. Its psychodynamics operates on the projective pole of the personality given above, and it can also be found in fetishists and anti-Semites. In summary, his experience reflects the psychodynamics described by Freud in the Schreber case, albeit with additions that cannot be easily demonstrated.

It is worthwhile to recall some reflections of E. Minkowski on this problem because of their simplicity and historical reality. This author emphasizes the therapeutic influence resulting from the fact that E. Bleuler used the word "schizophrenia" instead of "dementia praecox." His view is based on the fact that the term "dementia," to the extent that it represents an irreparable loss of psychic faculties, is destined to paralyze every attempt at treatment. When "dementia praecox" was talked of, because of its very designation, a negative therapeutic effect was exercised. On the other hand, with the introduction of the word "schizophrenia," irrespective of the interpretation of its symptomatology, therapeutic possibilities have been opened up—not only from a pharmacological point of view but from a psychotherapeutic approach. If it is believed that what one is faced with, as Minkowski states, is a deteriorated person, the patient inevitably becomes more and more deeply immersed in his autism. On the other hand, by interpreting his disturbance as a loss of contact with reality, the possibilities of psychotherapy are opened up. M. Bleuler correctly stresses how the clinical treatment and evolution of schizophrenia itself have changed in recent years.

The utilization of a more ample concept, such as *schizophrenic existence,* implies an advance similar to that indicated by Minkowski. It is then that one rapidly realizes that the fundamental psychodynamic difficulty that presents itself consists in *coordinating the symptom with the personal history of the patient.*

When one endeavors to approach this existence, it can be seen that it has two fundamental aspects, each of which contributes in its own way to forming the psychic picture. On the one hand, delusion appears, followed by the rest of the symptoms that we can appreciate. In our analysis of the patient's situation, it is very important to bear in mind these two points: first, the presence of the state of delusional mood, which we have already discussed and which is condensed into what Conrad termed "apophany." Basically, this refers to that change of aspect and significance which the world adopts for the patient as the fundamental root of the elaboration of his symptoms and, consequently, of the psychotherapeutic effort that is made.

The other pole of the picture presented by the patient is found in the theme. Among the classic psychiatrists, Gaupp directed his attention mainly toward the genesis of the theme, as had been done in the neuroses. On this basis, a number of nosological questions have arisen, questions that are as important as the relations between the schizophrenias, in the proper sense of the term, and the paranoid developments, in the sense that Jaspers utilized this expression. In any event, what must be borne in mind is that the delusion and other symptoms of the schizophrenia are found to be connected with the very being of the man or, rather, with his very existence.

As regards the themes of schizophrenics, we observe their election of themes of a general character. We could call these themes suprapersonal; they have as fundamental points of reference the problems of human existence in general, and they are not individualized. If they present themselves with the characteristic of anxiety, they also refer to the primary or primitive anxieties of the human being. What characterizes them is always their *intentional character* with respect to reality, that is to say, their need to elaborate other forms of evidence which are not those of the healthy. It has been said that such forms of evidence have only a subjective value and not an objective one. Nevertheless, one cannot neglect the distinctions that exist between reality as it presents itself from without, and reality as it is lived through or experienced inwardly: the differences sometimes appear ambiguous and, above all, are always subject to a process of concealment and clarity, according to the different situations experienced by the person. In the case of the patient, there seems to be established a struggle between the constitution of the reality of the "I," with its process of identity, and the constitution of the reality of the world in which the "I" is inserted. In the normal being, such difficulties do not exist. *Any psychotherapeutic action must take into account the habituation of the patient to this destructuration between the "I" and the world as two distinct realities which the disease establishes, especially in the most acute phases and even in the phases that have not been cured or have left some residues.*

With regard to the relationship that is established between the symptom and the mode of life proper to the patient, what must be borne in mind is the tendency to convert the symptom into an autonomous theme that dominates the whole of his life, manifested, above all, in his tendency to concede it both an absolute and general value that changes the structure of his insertion in the world.

This morbid existential process is produced by the conflict between the patient's subjectivity and that which surrounds him. Attention to this problem was drawn a long time ago by Sullivan, who considered it one of the fundamental pillars of his conception of the altered mental life. It is interesting to point out that the whole thematic morbidity of the schizophrenic refers, in general, to his relationship with the life of persons and not with the life of things. That is why authors like Binswanger, Storch, Zutt, etc., speak in these cases of a "pathology of confidence." It is precisely the recovery of this confidence, irrespective of the thematic deformations that are introduced into the life of the patient, that is fundamental for him. The aid of the psychotherapist can be extraordinarily valuable in such cases. Binswanger draws attention to the "monotony of the imaginary scheme" of the patient, up to the point that he compares it with the following description that Uexkull gives to the world of the animals: each animal has its surrounding or enclosing world; and although normal man is characterized by living in an open world, the patient, on the contrary, seems to enclose himself in his own world. But this should be taken only as a comparison, and it should not be forgotten that delusion does not constitute a fundamental difference between the healthy and the diseased person as compared to animals and men.

It is not necessary to stress the great differences in delusions in different patients, since in many of them they are tenuously held and in others they appear to be immovable. Every psychotherapeutic effort must start from the principle that the knowledge of truth in itself is not that which characterizes healthy human mental life, *but rather the freedom and the manner of approaching the ways to seek it. For this reason the human world of the healthy has such a diverse range of opinions.*

Heraclitus distinguished between the *Idios Kosmos* and the *Koinos Kosmos*—the first, the world of the isolated, as in sleep, and the second, the world of the person to the extent that he is related to others. The fundamental psychotherapeutic task consists in dismantling the paths that lead the patient to concede the general validity of what he mistakenly believes and to show him how to find the evidence and the values that his existence needs. Pathology, in reality, does not consist of autism, nor in the idea that the *Idios Kosmos* dominates the *Koinos Kosmos,* but in maintaining a dialectical relationship between both and based on a sane intersubjective relationship.

In synthesis, we are facing new points of view, *a new image of schizophrenia.* Thanks to the special manner of treating or managing the patients—or perhaps of mistreating them, as M. Muller says—what we call schizophrenia (or the mode of existence of the schizophrenic) has changed. Instead of the fatal course toward chronicity or dementia, intermittent outbreaks are seen, and those "catastrophic forms" which we saw in our youth are exceedingly rare. The residues seen in some patients are reactions to the past disease rather than intercurrent symptoms. There is a general rule which governs: the more residues are sought, the more they are found. Hence the advisability of abstaining from all analyzing psychotherapy, whatever its form, in this pernicious way.

M. Muller, in a monograph published more than forty years ago, asked why many schizophrenics make such spontaneous and unconscious efforts to eliminate the influence of the pathological in order to reach a neutral mood. In the past, the psychiatrist started from the base that he was apparently faced with an incurable disease, and the patient seemed as though enclosed in the mental space of his delusion. Psychiatrists and psychologists failed to ask themselves how the psychic dynamics of the patient operated, which would permit him to come to a more tranquil horizon. Thus, the function of present-day psychotherapy *is to follow the same path—i.e., to make it easy for the patient to establish his tranquil confrontation with reality and,* if this is not fully achieved, to reach a sort of compromise that will succeed in *repressing the symptom in its own ambiance and not convert it into the substance of his life.* How can this be done? By dismantling the delusional world as far as possible and, above all, the *dominion that it has over his existence*—in other words, aiding him in the task of repressing what it has not been possible to eliminate.

"Spontaneous cures" of schizophrenic patients within a year are more frequent than was formerly believed. M. Muller calculated that 30 percent of the hospitalized cases fell into this category. If the patients are well looked after, and treated with drugs and psychotherapy, the figure is, according to my own experience, about 60 percent; if less involved cases are included, it reaches 70 percent. When necessary, the patient may be hospitalized for a short period, at times for a few days or weeks. If one wishes to have proof of such possibilities, it is simply necessary to see how schizophrenia becomes attenuated as the patient grows older.

It is therefore important to initiate treatment as early as possible and to realize that the schizophrenic's enormous anxiety, which forces him, psychodynamically, to the creation of symptoms, is a flame that must be tempered as soon as possible. For this purpose, authentic therapeutic contact with the patient is needed, and it is essential to maintain this contact and *to ensure that it is well directed.*

Present-day psychotherapy starts with a greater knowledge of the structure of human existence than that which existed twenty years ago, as well as with a better knowledge of the phenomenological and existential structure of the schizophrenic.

That man is not a "thing" is obvious; but things and men belong to, or are immersed in, a world. In what respect are they differentiated? Man's world is constituted as he advances in life; he discovers that in the world there are things, but he discovers something more important: the dimensions of his existence.

One of these fundamental dimensions is that of time. The present moment is determined not only by what it is now, but by what every person has been and by what he can be. What he was constitutes part of a closed structure, but without forgetting that it is seen from the perspective of the present. A profoundly depressed patient does not see the smiling moments of his childhood or the happy moments of his youth. He sees only those of negative sign, or the sad moments, or those loaded with a feeling of culpability, without realizing that this perspective stems from the bad mood which dominates his present. The future is something that does not exist for him; if it did exist, it would be a chain of infernal moments. Thus everything—past, present, and future—is submitted to this cruel perspective. When the depressions pass, the waters return to their course. And what is their course?

In life there are men and things, with varied relations and with repetitive moments, with monotonous habits and creative moments —this is certain. I am not referring to the creation of a scientific or literary genius, but to the creation involved in giving a form to his future. The past signifies the experience with which he approaches that future. The future is like a geography of possibilities, and the present is always the site of the decisions. In the daily life of the normal man there are many commonplace hours, but there are also exceptional hours, as when he discovers the love of the person who is converted into his beloved.

Time, existentially lived, is both dilated and contracted. It is dilated when new men and new things are integrated into its existence

—men and things that need to be discovered in a gradual way, starting with their initial aspect, as in a process of *aleteia*. This *aleteia,* this new illumination that will also reach what is already known, presumes a dilation of the temporal horizon. One's own world is not given; it is discovered. On other occasions the horizon of our own world seems to narrow, to become opaque. We do not see the possibilities in front of us; on the contrary, it appears as if the vacuum was removing support of our existence from us. We do not see the possibilities—only the losses of what was; and on occasion there appears before us the frontier of death and disease. We can speak or write of death without feeling affected; we can even attend moribund patients, as though the crossing between the two existences, that of the dying person and that of the attending person, pertained to two different horizons, and so it is.

We could examine, in neuroses or in depressions, the peculiar modification that surmounts the diverse existential dimensions, but it is necessary for us to address ourselves exclusively to the schizophrenics.

The vital horizon of a schizophrenic existence changes dimensions and perspectives, more slowly or more rapidly, according to the acuteness of the outbreak. When a delusion begins, there are changes in the significance of the things and the persons surrounding the patient. In many cases it seems that only a sector has changed; but what *is* certain is that the vital horizon is disturbed, and that which constitutes its space is filled with images or even with possibilities that do not crystallize in images. Delusion has been compared to a dream. *Such a comparison does not approach reality,* although on some occasions it may seem to do so. The patient himself would like to be sure that the persecution which, for example, does not let him live is not real but only a dream. With greater frequency he accepts the fact that those new significations proceed from his own mood. For this reason, it is not a question of people who are known or even unknown, but of something interior that dominates him. When he was well, his perceptions, his reasonings, and his approach to the world demonstrated that he had the possibility of doing this. In this case, possibility means power. Now it is the other way around; it is "the otherness," "the other," which has the power. What is certain is that he is reached by the sudden pains of that state of experience which is established between the *being and the non-being,* between the "one" and his "alter ego"—in other words, madness.

True, something analogous appears to happen to other patients. Neurotic anxiety can be anxiety with respect to death, with respect to not being oneself, etc.; but when we describe these states, and the same occurs with the depressives, it is essential that we establish what is different in the case of schizophrenia. In neuroses and depressions it is always a matter of an "as if," as Vaihinger expresses it in his philosophy of the *als ob.* In schizophrenia, on the other hand, the dimensions of its subjectivity are really altered, and the personality is impoverished and emptied within, to the extent that it refers to the common reality—ours and that of the other types of patients. In the schizophrenic, the new dimensions of his existence are revelations about that existence itself, which, although they appear acutely and do not last long, leave their trace, a residue of this manner of becoming ill.

In some patients we already find special features in the prepsychotic period, when the disease has not shown any manifestations. In this *latent psychotic* state there already exists the difficulty of contact, the deficit in achieving, so that his existential structures and dimensions scarcely succeed in touching those of the person who lives together with him and is closest to him. The prepsychotic seeks the contact as though he were seeking aid, and at the same time he feels his useless attempt to achieve that existential contact. If he moves away, he seems to shut himself up in himself, frustrating his own effort. When anybody else or, still better, when the psychotherapist tries to cross those frontiers and overcome the isolation of the patient, the latter tends to encapsulate himself even more. If the other person's attempt succeeds, even partially, he feels it as if it were an insult, an act of force, as if it were a question of a mitigated form of the subjective experience, which in a full psychotic manifestation we would call thought-echo, theft, or intervention of thought. The patient very often reacts with ambivalent feelings and attitudes: on the one hand, he fears this contact; on the other, he desires it. The more intimate and personal the themes are, the more ambivalent his attitude may be. The psychotherapist needs to appreciate intuitively those causal existential situations, for if he does not perceive the situation and he intervenes clumsily, he can give rise to the molding of primary delusions in a state of germination and crystallize them in delusion of persecution, jealousy, etc.

The original defects of the existential contact can also evolve in other ways. For example, the patient washes his hands of and "buries" whatever in his life resembles the life of other people, and he gives himself over to his metaphysical or philosophical delusion. Perhaps, based on the patient and the moment, it is possible to break this enclosure, which, in turn, implies the inability to create the particular horizon required by every personal existence. It is impossible to help a schizophrenic to recover if he does not achieve the reorganization of every aspect of his existential horizon. In referring to the patient's corporal image, Burton says, "It is my view that no successful treatment of a chronic schizophrenic can occur without a reorganization of the body image."

I do not believe that Haley can say that psychiatrists possess a sort of unique capacity, one that is guided by textbooks, and I feel that they now know what the real life of the schizophrenic is, thus creating a mythology of schizophrenia instead of actually studying the behavior of schizophrenics. In my opinion, it is more true that Haley, Szasz, Ring, Laing, and others suffer from a mental hemianopsia in attacking this problem. This subject requires more space than I can devote to it here. Somatic medicine, which has existed for centuries, has not solved all its problems. To this very day, medical science diagnoses multiple sclerosis as a disease, without its etiology being known. Epilepsy is diagnosed even though there are cases that we could call cryptogenetic, although this expression is not now used. There are many mental diseases with a known etiology—as well as others, such as schizophrenia and depression, which are provisionally understood—about which there still remains much to investigate, although more is known about them every day (a noteworthy example is the recent knowledge concerning the biochemistry of endogenous depressions).

It is strange, almost senseless, to inquire whether the term "schizophrenia" should be abandoned without first reading the history of the disturbances and designations which have been utilized to describe these "mad people," even though that history goes back only two hundred years. Nor will much progress be made in proposing helpful models, which never satisfy anybody, if different approaches are not tried. To Hoffer's contention that the remedy consists in living "outside society," we reply that there are many people who do so. Less industrialized societies can do it with greater facility; it is still easier, in such societies, to find "schizophrenics at liberty." It is a commonplace error to say that schizophrenics are all those who have difficulties in life. In medicine, one speaks of symptoms, which are not useful except to describe how the schizophrenic existence is differentiated from what is not schizophrenic, and to bring to light, as much as one can, its structure (which is what this book is concerned with).

Lidz, Wynne, Jackson, Bateson, and many others state that schizophrenia develops in those persons whose families have undermined the family infrastructure, abandoning them in the middle of an affective aridity. I strongly believe that affective aridity is certainly the sentimental state that produces most bitterness, and that this bitterness leaves an indelible mark on the inner life of the person. I also believe that if a mother, for example, continuously calls her daughter a prostitute, the younger woman will think, on hearing a similar word, that the insult is directed at her. What I find difficult to accept is that on this basis alone, and without the presence of other *fundamental factors,* it is possible to succeed in transforming someone into a schizophrenic. Let me add something else: It was in Freud's time that the use of the expression "dementia praecox" was replaced by that of "schizophrenia." I do not believe that Freud agreed with this psychogenetic affirmation of what was then called "dementia praecox." These and many other "irrationalities" correspond to life's reality and they leave traces in the formation of the personality; yet they are hardly sufficient to trigger a schizophrenic mode of life or existence.

Although genetic studies demonstrated the influence of hereditary factors some time ago, we are still at the beginning. The same can be said of many somatic studies.

We forget *the pain and suffering of the parents of schizophren-ics*. I cannot say that the mothers or families of the patients are easy to manage or advise; but my counsel is rarely disobeyed when they are told clearly how the patient must be treated and what they must do with him. Moreover, clinical experience has shown that after the first five years of the disease, the likelihood that the symptoms will diminish is enormously reduced. When a patient has passed through an acute outbreak, or more than one, his psychotic activity gradual-ly becomes extinguished, and he substitutes for it a life style colored with the shades of the schizophrenic. An adequate family environ-ment decisively aids recovery.

In schizophrenia and in other psychoses and neuroses which have a natural tendency, that is to say, because of the evolutive line of the disease itself—as happens in so many other diseases—the dan-ger is not in judging the role of the *schizophrenogenous mother* but, rather, that the mother, father, or family will accept the rule im-posed by destiny. Passivity has many possible translations, one of which is *resignation,* and anyone who has dealt with grave neuro-logical forms knows very well what it signifies and what line of con-duct he must follow. Another translation is that of *limited activity* (and not for a fixed period)—thinking that temporality is not measured by the clock but by internal time, by the continued and successive action required by the presence of interior time.

Present-day progress in the therapeutics of many cases of psy-chosis, as in the field of schizophrenia, is as rapid and brilliant as in the field of depressions. What a great difference there is between the schizophrenics locked up like archeological pieces in museums that were once designated as lunatic asylums, retreat homes, and hospitals, and the present forms of psychiatric assistance. The point of view has totally changed. What is taken into consideration is not the influence of psychotherapy, sociotherapy, or pharmacotherapy themselves, but what is appropriate for the patient. Acute schizo-phrenic outbreaks can pass rapidly by means of adequate so-matic and psychotherapeutic treatment. I have said that, with some exceptions, the hurricane that seems to trigger some schizophrenics in their first episode does not always lead to dementia. The whole problem of the schizophrenic life style is there, and the whole secret of the aid to be given is found in this possible remission or attenuation of a demential process. The patient becomes more and more humanized through human contact. First, pharmacotherapy is helpful; then the transference which comes with the psychotherapy of schizophrenia is a factor which counters psychotic situations. Naturally, in this complex of circumstances, the family is involved, but it has no explicit reason to be schizophrenogenous. Quite the contrary.

Extensive experience in varying treatment centers allows me to write these concluding words. Interest is never lost if one continues to question oneself and, by means of such questioning, to seek to make one's knowledge more profound. In reality, what is madness, what is mental disease? What is the *reason of unreason,* asked the good Alonso Quijano, when it was experienced by Don Quixote de la Mancha?

THE ALCHEMY OF SCHIZOPHRENIA

Arthur Burton

I. THE LIFE-STYLE CONCEPT

The investigation of schizophrenia is in a sad scientific state. The colossal volume of its literature is a compensation for the little that is revealed by it, and directly contradictory theories sit side by side without strain. The treatment prescribed varies widely—from psychotherapy to special environments to electroshock therapy to psychosurgery to enormous doses of specific vitamins, and to yet others. But by and large the treatment is empirical or nonspecific. No one claims a cure for schizophrenia, but several say they can improve it, or at least maintain significant "lucid-free" periods from its ravages. Our particular bias is the psychotherapy of schizophrenia, for we believe there are a sufficient number of treated cases on record to prove the efficacy of psychotherapy, but of course under specific conditions. Even Arieti, who basically shares an organic pessimism about schizophrenia with others, occasionally sees value in applying psychotherapy to certain cases.[1] Schizophrenia is perhaps the only major area of psychiatry in which theoretical innovation has been put into a deep freeze. And, as we shall see later, Sigmund Freud must share some of the responsibility for this state of affairs. A century of Kraepelinian orientation toward schizophrenia has, in my opinion, led not only to a scientific dead end but also to the ultimate evolvement of the large state mental hospital which collected schizophrenics as one collects matchboxes. This was then used to populate even more elaborate hospital systems but, as with all such accumulators, they failed to understand the dynamics of the collection process.

Schizophrenia served many needs for the nonschizophrenic. But the ultimate outcome was to wall the patient off socially and make those responsible for his treatment become afraid to enter his world. All of the evolved therapies of schizophrenia in the mental hospital then became directly or indirectly ego-distancing mechanisms, so that the physician never had to finally confront his doubts and fears of the mysterium of schizophrenia. The flamboyant symptoms of schizophrenia brought smiles and uneasy laughter to the staff—as though they had the inside track on the patients' craziness —and the more they felt this, the crazier the patients became. Until recent years no one bothered to try to understand the symbolism of the flamboyance or to get to the heart of the matter of schizophrenia in a loving sense. We said that the patient had a "thinking disorder," lacked affect, and was furthermore "split" in some unexplained but serious way. Thus nothing could psychologically be done in the face of such vast postulated spoilage! When Harry Stack Sullivan, Frieda Fromm-Reichmann, Otto Will, Jr., and others appeared on the scene, patients *mirabile dictu* stopped being so crazy, and the number of improvements and discharges began to climb. One psychoanalyst with an optimistic attitude toward schizophrenia was often sufficient to change the outlook of an entire hospital milieu. Then the being-in-the-world of the schizophrenic became more comprehensible, and we were at last ready to extend our theoretical horizons.

In a certain sense the cure of hysteria was accomplished at the expense of the cure of schizophrenia. It is a natural creative act to exclude from the creator's field of consciousness all that is not directly relevant to the discovery he is making at the time. It has appeared to me that both Freud and Jung felt subconsciously that they could not attend to discovering both hysteria and schizophrenia simultaneously. Each in his own way was basically appalled with the experienced discrepancy between the hysteric's almost eager and passive aggressive acceptance of the therapeutic transference and the schizophrenic's violent rejection of it. Neither man was temperamentally suited to long-enduring nonparticipation on the part of the patient—and there were always Kraepelin, Bleuler, and others waiting in the wings with their bad prognosis. Spotnitz,[2] who also decries the retardation of the psychoanalytic understanding of schizophrenia, points out that Freud even enforced his ideas about schizophrenia by the dictum that "the analyst who undertakes to treat such a case has committed a practical error; he has been responsible for wasted expenditure of time and has discredited his method of treatment and he cannot fulfill his promise of cure."

When I talked to Jung about schizophrenia in 1958, he repeated his earlier published statement that it was some kind of toxin which began as a psychological condition. When I pressed him as to the nature of the toxin, he became irritable and cut me off. But when he was asked to speak at an international program on the "frontiers of knowledge" and the "humanistic hopes for the future," he selected schizophrenia as precisely the topic he wanted to discuss. He said then:

> The investigation of schizophrenia is in my view one of the most important tasks for a psychiatry of the future. The problem has two aspects, physiological and psychological, for the disease, as far as one can see today, does not permit of a one-sided explanation. Its symptomatology points on the one hand to an underlying destructive process, possibly of a toxic nature, and on the other—inasmuch as a psychogenic aetiology is not excluded and psychological treatment (in suitable cases) is effective—to a psychic factor of equal importance. Both ways of approach open up far-reaching vistas in theoretical as well as therapeutic fields.[3]

Jung wavered back and forth in his position on schizophrenia— he never went beyond his first book on the subject—and the quotation here represents his most liberal position. But Jung never for a moment gave up the idea of schizophrenia as a basically organic condition, and from time to time made concessions only to its psychological aspects. It is a puzzle why one so interested in myths and symbols, as Jung was, did so little with the greatest symbolic question of all time.

Arieti[4] similarly points up the shortcomings of Kraepelin, Bleuler, and the others on schizophrenia in the following way: "It is often said that Kraepelin was more concerned with the structure of the psychic phenomenon than with the content, that he was more concerned with how the patient thinks than with what he thinks. . . . The most important contributions of Bleuler were those related to his study of the process of association and disturbances of the affective life, the concepts of autism and ambivalence, and his interpretation of negativism." The rest of the schizophrenic phenomenology was apparently left bare.

Kraepelin and Bleuler succumbed to the old scientific pitfall of seeing only that which was relevant to their special thesis. Not only was schizophrenia not ready for a dynamic interpretation, but the neuroses were coming center-stage and psychotherapy was evolving as an entity. Consider for a moment the following intriguing description of hysteria:

> The hysteric may have, paradoxically, intense sexual desire and never achieve complete sexual gratification. The hysteric cannot be entirely gratified by his or her private phantom relationship and is yet unable sufficiently to forego the phantasy relationships to make way for the naked reality of an actual one, for no real relationship can be trusted not to be too disappointing. . . . Hysterics frequently say they have more real feelings in imaginary situations than they can experience in real ones.[5]

Can any scientist ignore the invitation that such a painful paradox offers? Add to this high intelligence, verbal ability, culture, affluence, attractiveness and dependency, and so on, which the neurotic brings to the consulting room, and the contrast with the schizophrenic patient is complete. Hysterics are by and large elegant people, and their treatment has a certain grace about it. The same cannot be said for the schizophrenic. The most convenient way of solving the problem, and the most self-acceptable, was prognosis. The claim of a good prognosis for hysteria and a poor one for schizophrenia, reinforced by the authority of Freud and Jung, was sufficient to divert attention from the latter for a century.

The thesis of this book does not come as a bolt out of the blue. It has been anticipated for years by Alfred Adler, Adolph Meyer, Harry Stack Sullivan, Lewis Hill, Ludwig Binswanger, and, more recently, by Ronald Laing. Possibly our contribution is to take that final leap into phenomenological faith which perhaps most of these men stopped short of. And the times force one to precisely such a leap. But more than that, the life-style theory of schizophrenia is linked with a more viable treatment method than other models afford. We would in all sincerity claim that the psychoanalytic treatment of schizophrenia succeeds insofar as the analyst quietly practices as a phenomenologist. It is not sufficient to merely make the bold theoretical statement. One must couple such a breakthrough with a set of operations that offer at least a modicum of improvement on past models. We believe we have made such a beginning.

The question of a cause of schizophrenia inevitably returns to a biological or tissue model as the primary one. This is of course the one most fundamental to medicine, the one we know best, and the one to which the word "cure" is fundamentally related. There is a good feeling of closure about the medical diagnosis and treatment of a disease—say, tuberculosis—which leaves all participants, including the patient, with the grand feeling that everything that can be done is being done. The pathogen, following the model of Koch, Virchow, and Pasteur, is conceived to be a bacterium, a virus, an inflammation, a trauma, an unregulated cellular growth, a protein molecule, and similar biological processes. A disturbance of the organization of functional systems of organs, or of the total expression of all organs as a working unity, or of the overriding motivation or biological purpose of the organ systems, reflected on the personal operative level, is most difficult to receive and accept. We have been impressed, for example, by how physically healthy neurotics in psychotherapy are. Indeed, it takes good organ health to be neurotic. The neurotic patients we have had in psychotherapy who came up with leukemia or some other fatal disease quickly gave up their neurosis, and the psychotherapy as well, to go about the business of being sick and dying. There is a paradoxical relationship between physical illness and mental illness.

The hard evidence for a genetic, biochemical, vitamin, or protein deficiency as a cause of schizophrenic is not as clear-cut as the proponents of this evidence believe. And even if such findings were specifically causal, there is always the question of their phenomenal or social repercussion, which involves entirely different layers of behavioral functioning. If we have learned one thing from fifty years of brain research, it is that no point-to-point phenomenal relationship exists between a neuron and its manifested social act. Schizophrenia has so diverse a patterning from patient to patient that it is hard to see how one universal physiological or biological cause can be applied to it. And, for all of the organic findings, schizophrenia grows apace, for no clinical method has effectively evolved from these findings. Lidz answers this question in the following way:

> Although the question of whether schizophrenia is basically a genetic, biochemical, or environmental problem certainly has not yet been definitively settled, our findings and theory lean heavily toward the environmental. However, as parents convey both, the genetic and environmental forces are not readily separated. It is possible that the poor family environments and also the disturbed ways of thinking and communicating noted in the parents are reflections of a genetically transmitted deficiency in the parents. Still, it appears to us that belief in a genetic or biochemical causation or predisposition to schizophrenia increasingly rests upon preconception and tradition, while evidence points to environmental and social factors. One of the major reasons for belief in a genetic predisposition, the supposed high concordance rates in identical twins, appears to have been discredited or, at least, seriously challenged by the studies of Tienari and Kringlen. Even if a clear-cut physiological or biochemical abnormality were found in schizophrenic patients, it might still depend upon faulty nurturant care in childhood. The disturbed lactate-pyruvate ratio that Gottlieb and his coworkers have found in schizophrenic serum may be related to the maternal care the patients had received, for they find

a similar abnormal ratio in the serum of monkeys Harlow had reared in isolation.[6]

It is conceptually harmful, and a result of the Judeo-Christian mind-body separation, to deny the functional and phenomenological by use of the organic. Even when paresis was discovered to be the result of a syphilitic spirochete invasion, it did not change the phenomenological manifestation of paresis when it did occur. It may well be that by a technique not yet discovered an organic cause of schizophrenia, perhaps in the cellular structure, may someday be found. But while we are waiting, society seems to have changed from a neurotic to a schizoid or schizophrenic one. Ambulatory schizophrenia, or petit-mal schizophrenia, as I call it, is now more the norm, whereas the hysteria of Freud is hard to find. The inevitable deterioration in schizophrenia which so much impressed Kraepelin, Greisinger, Bleuler, and others as the final stigmata does not occur today with such finality. When the state hospital began to be abandoned, the deterioration seemed to go as well. Schizophrenia was analogically the cancer of a century ago and, in one way or another, defined as a subtly insidious and unknown organic process that led univocally to death. The actual longevity is of course longer, and the death sometimes social rather than physical. And in both cancer and schizophrenia it is known that the "silent carriers" of the disease may never erupt and manifest themselves because as-yet undefined inhibitors cancel the behavioral posture and death actualization. The many spontaneous remissions in both cancer and schizophrenia are considered unexplainable miracles. Are they? Shulman says in this connection:

> Who becomes schizophrenic? Unless we are willing to assume a genetic deficiency, chemical disturbance, or a puppet-like reaction to the environment we must accept that the person who becomes schizophrenic exerts some choice in regard to his behavior. It is not only the actual situation in which he finds himself, but also the particular choice of response he makes to it that sets his feet on the path to schizoid behavior. The child must actually conspire with the environmental pressure to bring about a situation which leads him to schizophrenia.[7]

The possibility that a patient can "choose" his symptoms or psychosomatic disability is a foreign and violent one to medicine, which prefers to see the patient as a helpless victim of his pathogen. But those of us who work with the psyche on a deeper level understand how easily unconscious energy attaches itself to certain organs, or organ systems, and how such attachment makes sense to the patient in terms of his unsatisfactory life and its vicissitudes. Most schizophrenic somatization we have encountered centers around the head or brain, and delusions of a part of the head being missing, or bizarre feelings in the "workings" of the head (and the sex organs too, of course), are common. Why the head or brain specifically? Well, perhaps because our experience of our self and the ambient world is mediated through the brain, and the quality of that mediation is precisely what is involved in schizophrenia. In every instance of dis-ease a dynamic relationship can be found between the disease process and its host. In certain instances, the disease takes over or incorporates the life style, becomes the life itself; in others it represents more simply "a time out" from life. Thus asthmatics, arthritics, diabetics, epileptics, the migrainous, etc., can better be portrayed by their organic life style than by their blood chemistry or MMPI profile. Patients fear chronic diseases not so much because of the pain and ultimate death as for the need to change the modes of living they have spent decades building. We need a more apt term than psychosomatic, one that would more precisely describe the interaction of organ disease and the life style which erupts from it. We consider the term *body vita* more descriptive for this purpose.

It is, then, an artifact of our science rather than a reality that we seek an organic *or* a psychological basis for dis-ease, for the two are certainly one single phenomenon. Admittedly, a "magic bullet" is sought by Everyman, which is perhaps why mysticism is enjoying such a great vogue at present. But what if the truly great psychological pathogens of mankind, those producing dis-ease, are rather slow accretions of perception, habit, feeling, etc., over a lifetime, which deprive by an amotivational syndrome and by a loss of a certain vital quality of life? Adler was the earliest to sense that the interpersonal was not merely a numerical concept—how many friends one had—but the special quality of the friendship-net and the love and intimacy afforded by it that was the important thing.

The principles of schizophrenia offered here, while inclusive in nature, perhaps apply best to those schizophrenic patients we call ambulatory (petit mal) and who come to the office to be treated, or who at least do not stay very long in hospitals. The chronic schizophrenic with long years of state hospitalization is a special case because hospitalization has already layered him with so many additional peripheral values and conflicts. Furthermore, this hospital milieu has affirmed his schizophrenic self-concept, and he resents any interfering reinterpretation of his state of being. We can no longer be concerned with the hospital rubrics of *simple, hebephrenic, catatonic,* and *paranoid,* for these are artificial abstractions merely designed for the convenience of the hospital observer. The traditional diagnostic and prognostic values which flow from these classifications as *qualitative distinctions of being* do not exist for us in reality. Every schizophrenic is by definition at least potentially paranoid, potentially catatonic, potentially hebephrenic, and potentially simple. The true diagnosis is of course mixed! It amounts to what side of him the patient wants to present to the world (and to his doctor) at the moment and, indeed, what his doctor will allow the patient to reveal to him. The historical observers of schizophrenia were fascinated by what they called "deterioration," but we are fascinated by the schizophrenic who never makes it to the state hospital and who never deteriorates beyond the rest of us. We are convinced, however, that it is all-of-a-piece schizophrenia, and are not at all impressed by the so-called "process-reactive" continuum of schizophrenia. Upon closer and longer-term examination, every schizophrenic reaction turns into a process, and every process into a reaction. In the current state of our knowledge, the diagnosis and prognosis of schizophrenia do not permit us to label the patient as either process or reactive. Who among us has ever experienced the worst "process" kind of patient one day beginning to change, and then soon leaving the hospital without a conceptual rhyme or reason? And, per contra, we have seen "reactive" cases who make a rapid descent into social and hospital vegetation.

It would be fitting at this point of seeming confusion to ask for a definition of schizophrenia, for we could be accused of not talking about schizophrenia at all. Thus Stierlin[8] defines schizophrenia as "a disturbance in human development and adaptation whose characteristic features are brought to light by jointly applying three principles: differentiation-integration, adaptive reconciliation, and adaptive antagonism." By the first, Stierlin apparently means a certain unevenness in personal development; the second he defines as a peculiar weakness in energy, and in goals in relationship to one's world; and by adaptational antagonism he implies the defensive character of schizophrenia which is surprisingly *without gain.*

Arieti says that "schizophrenia is a specific reaction to an extremely severe state of anxiety, originated in childhood, and reactivated later in life."[9] It carries paleologic, affective, cognitive, and social psychopathological freight of a tall order.

Hill summarizes schizophrenia as

> a rupture, a dissolution of the ego, a shrinking of the ego, an invasion and taking-over of much territory, which did belong to the ego, by forces which are normally excluded from it. Subjectively, this is experienced as a catastrophic event of cosmic proportions. It is terrifying. Thought, feeling, and action are taken over; the patient is dispossessed of his own mind and body. Objectively, this panic arises as a response to some rupture of human relations or of the hope which the patient may have had of them.[10]

Spotnitz says that schizophrenia is

> an organized mental situation, an intricately structured but psychologically unsuccessful defense against destructive behavior. Both aggressing and libidinal impulses figure in this organized situation; aggressive urges provide the explosive force while libidinal urges play an inhibiting role. The operation of the defense protects the object from the release of volcanic aggression but entails the disruption of the psychic apparatus. Obliteration of the object field of the mind and fragmentation of the ego are among the secondary consequences of the defense.[11]

Sullivan's description of schizophrenia is diffuse, but in a single citation he said:

> The term *schizophrenia* covers profoundly odd events which are known to most of us only through what happens in our sleep; in our earlier years of life, a great part of our living was schizophrenia, but we have been carefully schooled to forget all that happened then. When a person is driven by the insoluble character of his life situation to have recourse in waking later life to the types of referential operations which characterized his very early life, he is said to be in a schizophrenic state. People who come to be called schizophrenic are remarkably shy, low in their self-esteem, and rather convinced that they are not highly appreciated by others. They are faced by the possibility of panic related to their feelings of inferiority, loneliness, and failure in living.[12]

To summarize these and similar definitions of schizophrenia in the literature, the agreed-upon manifestations seem to be (1) a peculiar diminution of affect, (2) a turning inward of object energy, (3) a small or larger hiatus between the person's cognition and emotion, (4) a kind of infiltration of the thought processes, (5) a loss of ego boundaries, (6) anxiety, phobias, projections, delusions, and somatizing, in various degrees, and, finally, (7) a complete turning away from the outside world to the self. The problem areas, one might say, are focused in drive mastery, affectivity, relational capacity, and thinking. The literature reveals that in childhood such patients were, by and large, described as good, clean, obedient, and adoring children, but also at times unique or strange. As adults they are more interested in ideals than action; they are not highly versed or interested in sex; they are more or less indifferent to money; and efficiency and progress as drives are beyond their ken. They are not organization men and do not administer or follow well. Values and meaning in life count heavily with them, to the point where we have in the past called them philosophers of existence or, more aptly, poets of existence. Above all, they give the appearance of being not unsocialized but asocialized people who will not play the social game.

The definitions of schizophrenia cited leave something to be desired. They give one the feeling that while speaking the same language they define different phenomena or different levels of phenomena. Once the obvious externals are left behind, it is extremely difficult to make a consensus of them. Thus the tendency of today's investigator of schizophrenia is to dump them all and make a fresh start. There is a growing investigational impatience in the field, and the avant-garde and radical ideas of Binswanger, Laing, and others on schizophrenia arouse interest everywhere. We have therefore in this book taken a further leap into theory which at first glance seems idiotic, if not actually regressive. But a sober second consideration reveals that any long-term psychotherapy or psychoanalysis of a schizophrenic person *pari passu* encounters—and attempts to change—the life-style aspects of schizophrenia. The proof of the pudding is in the treating!

Consider for a moment, and holding off the organic aspect of schizophrenia, the various psychological theories posited for schizophrenia in the literature: (1) the schizophrenic has a concealed bisexuality; (2) it represents a defensive neutralizing energy; (3) it involves defective ego boundaries; (4) it is a loss of ego feeling; (5) it is produced by repeated frustration; (6) it involves oppressive super-ego control; (7) it is a basic disruption of affective and emotional life; (8) it is a return to the pre-verbal mother-child relationship; (9) it represents a perversion of the maternal instinct; and, finally, (10) it involves a family communicational problem of double and other binds.

Alas, none of these, or even all of them, summatively, come anywhere near reaching the heart of the problem of schizophrenia. It is therefore necessary for us to attempt to reach beyond them to a more complex and meaningful description. The rise of schizophrenia seems correlated with the rise of Western culture. Along with removing man from the world of objects, as an object, and making him central to existence, giving him center stage, placing him above the naturalness of biology, came schizophrenia. We might in this sense claim that schizophrenia became a dis-ease of the consciousness of self, of the position of being his own sun to the earth, and, indeed, the greater that consciousness, the greater the possibility of schizophrenia. The dynamic ethic of repressive hysteria no longer suffices in a world beset by an even more desperate search for consciousness and feeling. This we would call not a consciousness but *the* humanistic consciousness. Caruso makes it clear that

> humanism in the service of total man toppled over into its own contradiction and disavowal and progress went into a terrifying decline; alongside a purely formal progress came the murder of liberty and human dignity, the extermination of the helpless, mass murder, total war, concentration camps, the atom bomb, all the vast misery and dread of this century. . . . At no time in history has man believed himself to be the absolute centre of the world quite as much as he does today; and yet at no time in history was he quite so relative, so powerless, so endangered.[13]

Our novelists, more than our scientists, have sensed the growing schizophrenic nature of modern man in this response to his centeredness. Albert Camus and, more recently, Alexander Solzhenitsyn have portrayed this philosophical dilemma best of all.[14]

Each one of Camus' heroes is critically faced with the problem of self. From Meursault in *The Outsider,* who cannot weep at his mother's death and who kills aimlessly without motive, to Dr. Roux, in *The Plague,* who, knowing that he will be infected with the fatal black plague, nevertheless stays and does his duty when other men around run from death, they are caught in the vortex of self and "other"—the fatal narcissism to "other"-dedication. For Camus and Solzhenitsyn, life has a special quality of paradox which makes the way men currently behave existentially *absurd.* These paradoxes are the strains between reality and the ideal, between art and materialism, between the actual and the absurd, between what men say and what they do, etc. Camus insists that the only true basis for being a humanist is to seriously consider suicide every single morning on arising. All the heroes in his books wander around in a schizophrenic autism and ambivalence and, as I described in an earlier publication, can be independently diagnosed by psychiatrists as having schizophrenia. Is it possible that we can learn something from these gifted and prescient writers about a theory of schizophrenia?

Phenomenological observations on schizophrenia which transcend the run-of-the-mill variety have been made by a number of people. Binswanger, for example, talks about the *inconsistency* and *disparateness* in the lives of such patients:

> The basic concept used in understanding what is called the schizophrenic existential pattern proves to be the notion of a breakdown in the consistency of natural experience, its inconsistency. Inconsistency implies precisely that inability to "let things be" in the immediate encounter with them, the inability in other words to reside serenely among things.[15]

What Binswanger is saying is that schizophrenia is such a torment because schizophrenics are unable to come to terms with the inconsistency and disorder of their experience, they cannot "let be," and they seek constantly for a way to reestablish order in their lives. They long for peace, for the laying aside of self, of dread, and long even for a kind of blazing death.

> The last way out manifests itself without exception in the formation of Extravagant Ideals that masquerade as a life-stance, and in the hopeless struggle to pursue and maintain such ideals.[16]

In speaking of the case of Lola Voss, Binswanger says:

> There can no longer be any talk of Lola's being in a position to give up the Extravagant Ideal of absolute safety, afforded by her language oracle, because here, as everywhere else, giving up the Extravagant Ideal means the bottomless anxiety of succumbing to the other side of the alternative. . . .[17] They persist in suffering because things are not the way they would like them to be, and persist in merely dictating the way they should be; which is to say, their mode of behavior is that of mere wishing and chasing after an ideal.[18]

Shulman says as well:

> What others have called poor ego functioning, poor drive control, and the emergence of the primary process is the schizo-

phrenic's careful inattention to those stimuli and perceptions that he wants to filter out and the consequent availability of illogic, unreason, illusion, fancy, etc., both as modes of perception and as modes of communication.[19]

He goes on to add that common sense, social participation, and the rules of life by which society operates interfere with his movement toward his chosen goal. He must isolate himself because we intrude on his privacy toward the Extravagant Ideal.

Cancro goes further:

. . . suggesting that we reject the disease entity approach to schizophrenia and substitute a fresher view. Schizophrenia is the reaction pattern or syndrome associated with a particular equilibrium achieved by the individual in response to certain classes of derangement that may originate in any sphere of his life, physiologic, psychologic, or sociologic. It is tempting to speculate that the time period during which the new stable equilibrium is being sought represents the acute phase of the syndrome and the time period after it is established represents the chronic phase.[20]

Sullivan is reported as having said that schizophrenia was a problem in self-esteem and that the life factors were paramount in causation and certainly in the cure.

Ronald Laing presents the problem in its special aspects in his unique way:

One finds that person who is entirely given over to a phantasy of something that can be searched for and found. He *is* only his own very searching. What one has is always not what one wants, and yet it is precisely the elusiveness of this want that one is unable to say what one wants, lacks, has not got, because what one wants (lacks) is precisely what one has not got. . . .

What is, what one is, what other people are, facts—this is not what is wanted. Those brute facts that cannot be eluded are repellent if not nauseating, disgusting, and obscene. This reality, so coarse, so vulgar, so fleshy, tends usually to be epitomized for the other: for the woman it is men, for the man it is women in their earthy aspects. . . .

But if a person's whole way of life becomes characterized by elusion, he becomes a prisoner in a limbo world in which illusion ceases to be a dream that comes true, but comes to be the realm in which he dwells, and in which he has become trapped.[21]

Hill comments, on the basis of his vast experience with schizophrenics:

But schizophrenia, the experience and the way of operating, can and does occur in many persons who are supposed to be physically ill, drunk, drugged, psychoneurotic, psychosomatic, or plain normal.[22]

And in another place he says:

An intended conclusion from this discussion is that schizophrenic patients, long before their acute illness, function in a fashion which shows that they have not developed in the manner of psychoneurotic and normal people in terms of a primitive pleasure principle, which comes to be interpreted and modified through experience with the environmental realities. They operate clearly upon some other principle, which supersedes and transcends the motivation which applies to us. They are interested in values and meanings which are not obvious to us. They have an extensive, systematic avoidance and system of denials by which they evade entanglements with the reality which is what makes life worth living for the rest of us. They are dedicated clearly to some unrealistic goal—at least, unrealistic to us. This leads to the statement of what has been obvious in all our approach to the schizophrenic: Schizophrenics, as compared with other people, are extremely serious and are interested in meaning: they are trying to find some unifying principle, trying to find some sort of peace, symmetry, or harmony in the world. Since it is not in the real world, they look for it elsewhere.[23]

Before taking up the implications of these observations, it is necessary to consider a stumbling block which inhibits our understanding of schizophrenia as we phenomenologically know it. This is the central question of what constitutes the meaning and importance of a psychosis. We have in our professional experience spent many hours with schizophrenic patients who we were convinced were not psychotic—not at any rate as a psychotic process—and if they ever had been psychotic, they were so only on the most transient or borderline basis. The earliest observers of schizophrenia were, I believe, overly awed by the departures in reality testing that schizophrenia affords, and they became obsessed with the distinctions to be made between neuroses and psychoses. Innumerable hours have been spent in various staff conferences making just such decisions. And why not? If the psychosis is an organic-deteriorative process, with an ultimately bad prognosis, then quite properly it makes a difference whether the patient is neurotic or psychotic. We have been a participant in a thousand mental-status examinations in which the response to the everlasting question, "Do you hear voices?" was sufficient to qualify the patient as psychotic. But in this day of quick hallucination, marijuana, mystical states of consciousness, and sensory deprivation, and in the face of our newer understanding of the distortions of perception, hearing "voices" is not necessarily diagnostic of a psychosis.

We sometimes hedge by calling psychoses "transient" or "borderline," but a psychosis, if it exists, must be more than a departure in reality testing. It must represent a new outlook on the self and on the world, and must be a *new* personality evolvement or a different form of evolvement. One may also perhaps be psychotic in one tiny area of the personality, or merely on a part-time basis, but a diagnosis of psychosis is always presumed total. The implication of at least the older psychiatric textbooks is that once a hallucination is present, the entire personality is corrupted. I do not believe this is true.

Modern psychology teaches that reality serves only the nuclear core of existence, and since the human situation is never without care, reality is always more or less bent. The police arm of society should not be the selective instrument by which such cases become located. The judgment of the reality distortion, and its meaning, always come from the outside, from a spectator, and one who is presumably better able to know what reality is. But does he? Whose reality is being served in such instances? And today reality is itself a philosophical question, just as whether adults always know better than their children what is good for the children.

The following statement was written by James O., a 21-year-old patient of ours, who came to treatment because instead of continuing his university education as his most successful father desired, he only felt comfortable drumming, which he also sometimes did in a rock band. His mother, to whom he was intensely attached, had died several years before, but he had never mourned or accepted the fact of her death. He hostilely refused to follow in the footsteps of his father, whom he saw as existentially unhappy in life. He had been a moderately heavy pot, speed, and LSD user but, at the time of coming to therapy, had given drugs up as not the answer. By all available diagnostic criteria—social functioning, Rorschach Test, psychiatric evaluation, and symptom manifestation—he could not be considered more than conventionally neurotic. The university he attends has thousands of students like him. But now consider what he says:*

> By means of a kind of filter, I'm not altogether here—there's a kind of delay mechanism in my head, through which everything I experience has to go. I have a feeling it was, you know, originally set up as a defense, to protect me from things that would hurt me, because I could, I could protect myself from what was trying to harm me by, by delaying its impact and by kind of rationalizing it. That's, that's what the filter does. I think the filter takes the form of a voice. In kind of mild instances—I could be taking a test, and I'd be wanting to do well, and all the time in my head I'd be hearing, "You got to do well. You got to follow directions. Try hard. Do well. Pay attention. Read all the directions." And this kind of thing. I'd be hearing so much *noise* in my head that I really never did all that well. The, the voice would be giving me so much advice that I, I couldn't really participate in the test. I was never really tested so much on what I *knew* as on my, you know, ability to be there and actually be taking the test; 'cause really I wasn't all there and taking the test. Most of me was just listening to

* All italicized words are the narrator's.

this voice telling me to do this and do that, and I could hardly, you know, relax enough to just read the question and *do* it.

I think, though, where it, you know, it served me well is kind of the reason it came into being, too, if . . . if I were undergoing a kind of painful experience, this filter would kind of lessen the pain. I can remember . . . my parents . . . doing something that would hurt me, or, well specifically like my sister. I can remember, her beating me up and, like, the filter was like a mature voice, a rational voice, a voice of reason—kind of reminds me of my father—and it, it told me that, you know, she's just, physically beating you up, but that doesn't matter, like, 'cause you know what's happening and you know she's being childish and that you're right, you've got right on your side, and so it really doesn't matter. I think the voice was always telling me, you know, it doesn't matter; tell me things like, "Don't show how you feel. Don't let 'em know. Don't let them know how you feel. That's your strength." And so the voice was kind of like a guide, a guide in the world.

When I was little I used to talk to myself a lot. I have the feeling that the filter, this kind of voice, is somehow related to that; 'cause eventually I think I was mostly coerced or embarrassed out of talking to myself—and so I, the myself I talked to and held the conversation with, you know, kind of became internalized and, . . . Seems like I really didn't have to talk to *it* any more: it wasn't necessary for me to bring a conversation up with me; it was like, it was *there* as a constant source of advice. But wow, right now I really find that, uh, constant advice just a total drag. It doesn't, doesn't *allow* me to be where I am, it doesn't allow me to really experience what's, what's going on. And I guess if my world was always full of painful experiences which—I'm beginning to see it really was, a lot, as a kid—it was a good, it was good, because it softened, it softened that world. Reminds me of a friend of mine who always used to wear, who *needed* glasses, but when he was in the city he, like, wouldn't wear his glasses at all because everything, all the corners and the grayness and the drabness was kind of softened by not wearing glasses and so, like, he'd only wear them when he went out into the country, and when there was something to see. Some, somehow, you know, my voice, voice in my head, it, softened painful things.

The problem with it *is,* it is, it's on *all the time!* And, uh, you know, there are good things that are happening to me, too, and the reason I really feel like fighting it now is because I, I really feel frustrated in not really being able to get into the *good* things that'll be happening to me. I can really see it clearly in drumming: I can't get into the feeling at all and really make *any* kind of music if there's a voice telling me in my head, "Play well. Get into it. Feel it." I mean, the voice can be telling me kind of the things that I really should be doing, like, you know, the voice'll say, "Don't think, feel." But just the fact that I'm, I'm *saying* that to myself, it, it, it makes it *impossible* to feel, and to play, 'cause I, I'm, what I'm doing is *telling* myself to feel and to play and so, like, it's just a constant barrage of that noise, it doesn't let me get into it.

I find the times when I really *am* playing music I feel really good; I feel, I don't know, what feels to me like Superman, compared to the way I usually feel. I just really feel on top of it, I really feel good inside myself. And that's rare. But when it happens, there's no voice there, I'm, you know, I'm *quiet* inside. Quiet doesn't mean just kind of passive, I, 'cause, my, the music I play a lot is kind of violent. It just means I'm all there; I'm experiencing it, I'm not, it doesn't have to go through the censor, I'm not, hearing, you know, this voice.

It's really a kind of a dull voice, you know. There's nothing really that inherently attractive about it. I remember reading *I Never Promised You a Rose Garden.* And at least, you know, the voices she hears are kind of, seem a bit more creative, they're, they're part of a story of a kind of magical world. That seems a lot more attractive than my voice.

I now kind of see this filter as a real, you know, enemy I've got to defeat, if I want, if I want to enjoy myself, if I want to live. And—the orientation I have toward fighting things is to mobilize plans; out-think my obstacles. Like I never really had that much talent, I figured, you know, for the school work I was doing, but I'd really organize the work I did a lot, and just spend hours and hours at it, you know, I'd . . . I'd out-think the whole, the whole situation. But that. . . . Doing that is, won't work against, when against, this filter. In order to give it up I've just got to give it up, but I can't. . . . To *tell* myself, "Give it up," is, is working with the filter.

Somehow, it reminds me a lot of the final stage of Buddhism where you have to . . . . Well the end product of Buddhism is to give up all desires and the final step is to give up the *desire* to give up desires. As long as, as long as you *desire* to give up desires, you're, you're not there. It seems like as long as I'm desiring to give up this filter, that's basically the same process as the *filter*. My thinking of stop, stop the noise in my head: that, the voice that's saying that is the voice of the filter! So I just have to stop even *saying* that. And, it just seems to happen when I relax, when i'm just feeling real good. Well, that's all right. The way for it to shut up is just to feel good. It's a lot neater than my usual rational-attack plans.

Like I said, the filter now works in every situation. I don't think I *created* it for every situation but . . . once you start it, you know, even if it's just to protect yourself, it works *all the time!* Like I know I've repressed all kinds of things that have happened to me when I was a kid. But it's not like I just repressed those events. In the process of doing that, I repress smells of the woods, repress my, my seeing, I can't, I don't see a flower, you know the way anybody can see a flower. There's too much thinking there, too much of the filter there to really see it. I'm sure with my music, too, I really don't, hear, here very much. I notice the difference sometimes when I'm stoned, and the voice isn't there. Everything just seems so mystical, I see things so clearly, there's no noise, I just, you know, a flower is a flower, and a chord is a chord, and, a smell is a smell, and it's so *profound* and overwhelming that it seems there must be something magical about it! There's nothing really magical about it, it's just a normal smell, I think and a normal piece of music, and it's, it's what's normally there, only I'm not, filtering it out, I'm not, not heaping all my junk upon it; and just letting, letting those sensations come into me is, a, the few times it's happened it's been a really moving experience. 'Cause it's just so much different from the way I normally experience the world. I don't know when, when the filter's gone, and. . . . Eventually it sure is gonna be!

I guess on a larger scale, you know my whole life that, with the filter going, you know, protecting me from the whole thing, it, there's no meaning there. It's, uh, it's all happening, but, uh, it's so bland, so. . . . All the guts are, are out of it, it's, it's

> filtered, it's, it's not a strong diet. And like I have an appetite for a lot more. And to try—physically *try* to fill myself up, to try to fill that appetite is antithetical to, to filling it up. Somehow I've just got to, relax and, uh, it'll be filled up.

Twenty years ago, on the basis of this document alone, the patient would have been diagnosed as psychotic. Today I am not so certain. Indeed, all evidence beyond the statement itself, including projective tests, psychiatric examination, and 100 hours of psychotherapy, lead away from such a conclusion. His social adaptation is relevant to his age, place, and time; he demonstrates love and intimacy with his girl friend; he is now making progress toward his career, reveals some musical talent which he is acting upon, has never been antisocial or a behavior problem, has no other delusions or hallucinations, and has appropriate anxiety to his human situation.

Regarding the psychoses, Cancro says:

> When we say a patient is psychotic we mean in practice that he cannot function in socially adaptive ways. The inherent limitation of this basically social conception is that any social behavior which deviates radically enough is considered psychotic. One can be psychotic without being schizophrenic, and one can be schizophrenic without being psychotic. It is not that unusual to find non-hospitalized schizophrenics who are able to function quite adequately.[34]

It is schizophrenia *as a psychosis,* not schizophrenia as the phenomenon, which has retarded the understanding of schizophrenia. It is not the fact of the primary process and the primitive departures from normative mentation which deter us, for the same behavior occurs in "drug freakouts" in college youth and these mobilize us to action. I would insist that it is the definition (and history) of the concept of psychosis which deters us. A psychosis is something we want little of because in some way we perhaps fear the corruption of our own reality from the psychotic patient. There is in all of us a certain hidden need to be crazy—to go beyond the rules. And, indeed, the psychotherapy of every schizophrenic patient carries just this temptation. The concept of a psychosis now lacks precision; it is judged by the strength of the impulse underlying the behavior manifested, its social adaptation qualities; and it deters therapeutic effort as either useless or dangerous. Uncontrolled mania is the historical image of the psychosis.

The Rorschach Test is for us the method *par excellence* for assessing inner reality perhaps because we have administered thousands of them in the widest variety of clinical situations. What do we find? We have been chagrined and disturbed to find, as more than a rare occurrence, the most perceptually deviant Rorschachs in people who not only function reasonably well but have great social and economic responsibilities. One such person was each month responsible for millions of dollars of hardware missiles for our defense program, but according to his Rorschach he should have been in the closest mental hospital. Frank Barron found something similar in his assessment of some of the world's great artists and writers.

Psychosis is a kind of *post hoc ergo propter hoc* affair, and our advance prediction of who is to become psychotic is rather poor. Forensic psychiatry reveals that men of good faith and equally fine training disagree in the courtroom as to when a person is psychotic, often citing the identical evidence. We cannot deny a certain behavior in patients who have been called psychotic. It certainly has its non-adaptable aspects. But labeling behavior this way is now a handicap rather than a help to the cure, for it gives a false sense of confidence of the degree of understanding involved. It also has its non-humanistic properties and creates a special class of people who are finally segregated and, in Hitler's regime, put to death. The sociological evidence furthermore reveals that intelligence, beauty, affluence, skin color, and social and professional position reduce the probability of being called psychotic. The broad bi-modal diagnostic distribution of neurosis and psychosis is not only overly coarse but seems to have lost its clinical usefulness.

In this contribution, schizophrenia is not for us a psychosis *or* a neurosis; it just is. But the behavior manifested by the schizophrenic is certainly different at times from what we call usual or normative. The question then becomes: different in what way? But we refuse to use categories to answer such questions. Categories about a patient are always sicker than the patient. By looking at the problem phenomenologically we can perhaps leap the historical chains which have bound and categorized schizophrenia and place it closer to its individual (and social) meaning and purpose.

All psychoanalysis is posited on the assumption that the patient has an unknown "secret" that is doing him harm—taking a toll of him. Freud found this "secret" in repressed pleasure, and to this Jung added a dimension of mythical universality which he called archetypal. For the schizophrenic this "secret" was believed to be more primal, more urgent, more complex, and more affective. The evolvement of psychotherapy was faced with the problem of finding the most practical and efficient way of reducing the "secrets" of the patients. Why was it, then, that Freud latched onto the pleasure principle as the *bête noire* of psychologically conflicted people? Freud had convincing clinical and personal reasons, but Caruso interprets it this way:

> The reduction of all works of man to the pleasure principle was based on the fact that the pleasure sphere is the oldest tangible stratum of human development. From this Freud concluded that all the strata of human existence are causally determined by this oldest layer. This was the fallacy in his philosophical thinking.[25]

It was Adler who first sensed that the "secret" of the patient—actually of all people—was perhaps of a different order. He found it in the "social interest" and "social organization" of people rather than in the id. From this grew his idea of a "central purpose" in the lives of people, which he later replaced by the concept of "life plan," and finally by the term "life style." K. A. Adler, his son, describes what a life style is:

> The style of life, while influencing all its component parts, is not simply the sum of its parts, but generates its own unique quality in the course of its development. It also has a self-checking, built-in safeguard, precisely because any manifestation inconsistent with it must be rejected, or re-checked for its

validity, or the assessment of the life style must be revised by the therapist. This concept is the most definitive statement thus far in the field of ego psychology for the understanding and treatment of human character and behavior in all their seeming contradiction.[26]

And Alfred Adler, *pere,* said, "The nervous individual formulates his style of life more rigidly, more narrowly; he is nailed to the cross of his narrow, personal, non-cooperative fiction."[27]

Now, a life style is in a way an unsatisfactory concept from a rigidly scientific point of view, and some of Adler's observations on life goals seem teleological and self-servingly pragmatic. But it is necessary to find the personality structures which best fit wherever one can. And Adler's system of psychotherapy, based on his principles, is as good as any of record. Adler is certainly correct when he says that one's self is the basic motive of the personality —i.e., that no sensation, percept, feeling, etc., has value unless it can be interpreted against a framework of social interest and meaning. The process of growth is one of self-organization, which, when organized, feeds back, by sensation, percept, and feeling, a set of signals to the total organism. The organism then makes *human* sense of itself and develops a philosophy of existence. It then centers its selective perception around this conscious and unconscious philosophy of being.

The purpose of *Homo sapiens* is not to survive but to experience. The generalized and abstracted fear of death of the species produces an overdetermination in the social and behavioral sciences on adaptation and survival, thereby ignoring those many instances where life is surrendered for a higher non-biological motive or where adaptation is ignored. We sometimes call such people heroic, but this begs the question. We have difficulty countenancing people who are not like ourselves in this regard, and the possibility that survival is not the be-all and end-all of existence comes as a shock to some. The new community suicide rescue services now so prevalent everywhere are backed up by such an unconscious need to maintain survival in everyone at any cost. And alternate life styles are met with surprise, bewilderment, and downright hostility, as reactions to the college dropout and hipster reveal.

Families monitor the evolving life styles of their children and shape them in their own primal image. The reinforcements here are both subtle and complex, and love and hate become the vehicle of the proposed model. But what can be expected to occur if a child, by reason of genetic structure, temperament, organ weakness, or infantile deprivation, cannot meet the life-plan demands? What if his family deters or interferes with the new organization of self which clashes with the family life style? Obviously, the self-organization becomes heavily defensive, falls out of harmony with the indigenous self, and feelings of dishonesty, strangeness, and unreality begin to develop. The self goes underground and lives largely on under-life. But a price has to be paid for the tension between the ever-widening conscious life and the unconscious one. This most often is an evolving apathy and dissociation that serve to blunt the sharpness of experience and its hiatal pain.

A "life plan" is not such a far-fetched concept at all. Miller, Galanter, and Pribram[28] speculate that electronic computers are guided by a concept analogous to a life plan, although computers indeed cannot plan their own life. By computer life plan we mean any hierarchical process which can control a sequence of operations performed. The computer neurosis, therefore, becomes the failure or inability of that sequence.

The study of behavior has glossed over the manner by which the character constants are formed in the individual. Freud made a valiant attempt at this, and we now recognize the orificial contributions to the personality he described. But no study exists in which the formation of the life assumptions that back up the life plan selected are described. We ascribe to habit formation a power which more reasonably belongs to the pull of existential need and thrust.

Because repression does its work so thoroughly, we never become aware of the fact that each child lays out his own life plan and then proceeds by learning and experience to structure it into a life style. His cognitions, perceptions, and even feelings are then selectively made syntonic with that style and its elaboration. We see its work most microscopically in the patient; but the non-patient struggles just as mightily with his habits, interests, styles, customs, rewards, and punishments as does the patient. What is definitive in later adult character is not an early sexual trauma or its equivalent, but a nuclear life plan which struggles for definition and evolvement. It may perhaps even have some sort of genetic quality upon which it builds. The neurotic insult then becomes a severe damage to the life plan rather than a sexual or pleasurable deprivation as such. More than we know, the vast majority of children handle such deprivations without damage to their adult character structure. But they are unable to tolerate a serious interference with their loving destiny and their mode-of-being, as their conscious and unconscious structure it, and sit later as a homing beacon monitoring it.

The so-called generation gap, the differences between father and son which the sociologists now stress with so much vigor, is not so much a struggle between two temporal worlds as it is between two life styles. We must not forget that not so long ago schizophrenia was called dementia praecox and was considered a disease of adolescence. Adolescence is the crisis time of life when a life plan is effectuated and a life style demanded for work, love, and procreation. Youth takes life and death more seriously today and demands more personal fulfillment than it did in other centuries. Camus' ultimate message was to rebel—and rebel they do. But social and political rebellion has now primarily turned to "soul" or inner life rebellion, and to finding ways of coming to terms with the imaginative self. In this the growth of schizophrenia in culture plays its part.

Art has a way of leading the study of man because it does not bind the imagination in the way that science does. The outer and often lunatic fringes of art sometimes offer verities which only become clarified much later. There is also an art in science, particularly in theory building, which not many scientists acknowledge. In this connection surrealism and non-objective art shattered all conceptions of reality when they first appeared on the scene. Their social purpose was most unclear, and they were at first ascribed to a band of willful men, or perhaps to a group of madmen. But Camus has this to say about surrealism, drawing upon André Breton, the father of surrealism, for his gospel:

> Incapable of accepting the fate assigned to me, my highest perceptions outraged by this denial of justice, I refrain from adapt-

ing my existence to the ridiculous conditions of existence here below. Surrealism is "a° cry of the mind which turns against itself and finally takes the desperate decision to throw off its bonds." It protests against death and the "laughable duration" of a precarious existence. . . . This surrealism places itself at the mercy of impatience. It exists in a condition of wounded frenzy; at once inflexible and self-righteous, with the consequent implication of a moral philosophy. Surrealism, the gospel of chaos, found itself compelled, from its very inception, to create an order. . . . Whoever refuses to recognize any other determining factor apart from the individual and his desires, any priority other than that of the unconscious, actually succeeds in rebelling simultaneously against society and against reason.[29]

Schizophrenics have a "secret" goal in life, and this is the secret of their "narcissistic neurosis." The secret is that they will not normatively participate in the paradoxy of the *Absurd* world, and to do so is, in any event, beyond their tolerance. The concept of *paradox intolerance* is for us basic to the formation of schizophrenia. The paradoxy tolerance of some people in our culture is much less than others, for reasons yet unknown, and the ability to make a positive out of a negative is severely impaired in them. The original sin of the family double bind is that the child is taught by his family that there are no paradoxes in the family, while at the same time it reveals them covertly. One such family we worked with almost fell apart because the identified patient, a seven-year-old son, quietly stole money from his mother's purse. Theirs was, they said, a truly Christian home, and thievery had no place in it. But what soon became painfully apparent in the family therapy was that both the father and the mother, in the desperate economic need to "make it," were covertly using their morality for narcissistic purposes, at the same time denying to their children that such practices existed. Why shouldn't our young patient share in their spoils? And, of course, the more he stole, the wider the family split apart, for it could not survive in the old dishonest way. What makes schizophrenia so hard to treat is precisely that the patient is lined up against his family's and society's paradoxes. Indeed, successful psychotherapy of schizophrenia involves the task of helping the patient first see that such paradoxes do exist, and then showing him a different and more honest way of living with them.

Lidz and colleagues have studied the families of schizophrenics about as thoroughly as anyone we know.

> The theories which have guided our investigations and also those that appear to us to result from them lead away from the conceptualization of schizophrenia as a clear-cut entity to consideration of an aberration of the developmental processes—a failure to achieve or maintain a workable integration with retreat into asociality and an inability to participate in the logic and meaning systems of the culture with attempts to realize conflicts by altering the internalized version of the world without due consideration of reality testing.[30]

The question then becomes: What would force a child to give up his orientation to the social realism of his time? We cannot believe that any single form of family structure can produce this. We cannot believe that the so-called schizophrenogenic mother can do this by herself. We do not believe that even the most serious maternal deprivation experience of the Spitz variety can do this by itself.

We do believe, on the other hand, that in some way, not yet completely understood, the child receives a covert mandate from the family to rescue it from its paradoxes and later extends this mission to all society. It becomes his task to make the family philosophically and morally plausible. And society becomes the depriving mother and he is the child ordained to rescue that Absurd society. This is his Extravagant Ideal. If that society can actually be changed, as it was, for example, by Saint Theresa of Avila or St. John of the Cross, both considered schizophrenic in the psychiatric literature, or, say, by Abby Hoffman, as youth in rebellion, then paradoxy intolerance as schizophrenia does not apply in that individual life. If it cannot, as is the almost universal rule, then an entire revision of the self organization becomes necessary, and in the direction away from the social Absurd.

The core problem of schizophrenia is not autism but ambivalence. The positing and negating of behavioral alternatives is a regular and persistent feature of the human interaction with such a person. The small ambivalences—say, to go out on a date or even to read a certain book—must mirror the greater ones which lie underneath their full awareness. This may be put as Kierkegaard's Either/Or dilemma or Shakespeare's "to be or not to be." For some people the Either/Or becomes the basic dialogue of life, which eventually replaces in an obsessive way the living itself. The *idea* of action replaces the possibilities of action itself. And, in the schizophrenic, this takes the extremest form of catatonia, paranoia, and hebephrenia. To not make choices, to not act, to be besotted by thoughts—to ambivalize everything—leads to a social stasis which the observer must distinguish by a special clinical name. And when such ambivalence occurs in the momentous and loving decisions without which no life can function, then the person has found the most thoroughgoing negativism and divorcement that life affords.

In a more metapsychological cast we might say that some people are more involved with an inner paradisaical archetype than others. All people, of course, seek nirvana or heaven or what-have-you in one way or another, and satisfying this need is the bulwark of every religious system extant. While most people are content to, or have to, wait for it in the "afterlife," a few demand it here on earth. Now, my use of paradise must not be interpreted in the biblical sense but, rather, as a need for a special world without paradoxes and Absurdity. Personal paradise is a hypothetical life situation where each person can creatively express himself openly, directly, and honestly, and come to fulfillment without double-binds, games, hidden agendas, and complexes. The world of ideals comes closer to the world of reality and without having a saving Jesus, Buddha, Moses, or Muhammed. Such modern approaches to the paradise archetype are seen in certain aspects of the encounter group movement, youth drug communes, and the "Jesus freak" phenomenon, among others.

My contention is that the person who ends up with the appellation "schizophrenic" is in some way more imbued with the need to find that paradise for himself, that is, he not only needs to, but has to. Such archetype is more central to his being, and he cannot bind the aggression and love paradox involved in 57 murders in one

week in New York City alone (July 13–20, 1972) at the same time
as the most successful Campus Crusade for Christ happening ever
known (Dallas, Texas). The peculiar juxtaposition of sweet love
and murderous hate, its Absurdity, in contemporary society is a
phenomenon which not every child masters, and the inner capabili-
ty to tolerate such paradoxes as adults varies widely. In some whose
paradox tolerance is extremely low, and the paradise archetype
need supremely high, an adaptation must be made to the dialogue
of the inner tensional strain and the exigencies of the outer world.
The existent phobic structure of depression, obsession, paranoia,
etc., is then called into play and a new mode-of-being in the world
may be created which we then call psychopathological.

When the possibilities of fulfilling the paradise archetype become
totally closed, when the tolerance for the social paradox and Absurd is reduced to zero, then the person is faced with only the
Either/Or metachoice or of actually suiciding. Falling into this dilemma is more simply accomplished than most non-schizophrenic
individuals can appreciate.

One of the surprising findings of the use of the mind-expanding
drugs has been how quickly and easily one can become schizophrenic—give up the basic parameter of reality and reason. One
has only to systematically refuse to accept the idea of progress and
pleasure to find that the whole social world begins to fall apart. The
sociopath can give up progress, but cannot divorce himself from
pleasure; the schizophrenic eventually yields both.

Of course, it becomes a question of why a person with such latency
does not become monastic, ascetic, or hermitic—why he gives up
his persona in such (to us) bizarre ways instead of going to a monastery or its equivalent. Well, many do. But the answer seems to be
that in former centuries this was just such a probability, but the evolution of psychiatry as a response to newer social needs makes it
no longer feasible and the population of monasteries is falling. Culture has restricted such formal social modes of dropping out while
generally encouraging the chemical and psychopathological ones—
it provided the mental hospital in place of the monastery. Timothy
Leary very early recognized this modern social dilemma and
thought that he had found the solution in LSD, which he genuinely

believed to be nonharmful. Chemistry is pernicious: it discourages radical changes in life style because a point is eventually reached where the easy joy of the chemical discourages the strenuous effort required by a reasoned alteration of a way of existence. Most young people prefer pot or meditation to psychotherapy—and easy transactional analysis (Berne) to difficult psychoanalysis. Valium, Equinil, etc., are prescribed with unusual abandon in today's world for lives that cannot be lived, but they merely result in preserving the psychic status quo. Are they not in this sense pernicious? It is historically interesting that the Adlerians were the first to grasp the importance of such factors in the lives of patients and, of course, we can understand why Freud could never accept Adler's viewpoints. Consider, for example, the following quotation from an Adlerian:

> In varying degrees, the factor of hopelessness is always present. It is the common denominator in schizoids or schizophrenics. This is caused by their despair of ever being able to be of significance in the real world. Actual schizophrenia may, in fact, be crystallized in a patient when he feels completely checkmated by a real life problem. Adler considered this hopelessness so characteristic and so important an element in the development of schizophrenia that he said, "We could probably, by systematic discouragement, make any child into a person who behaves like a schizoid."[31]

We have too long ignored the special family and social position of the schizophrenic and, at any rate, we have denied causality to states of being because we have sought the pathogen in other directions. We sought a virulence which did not seem to be found anywhere in day-to-day living, but which turns out to possess just such properties. But the fact that the psychotherapy of schizophrenia uniformly uncovers the lower forms of paradox tolerance in these patients, and can alter them and the schizophrenia in most of them, gives credence to the possibility that the greatest psychic pathogen of all is the life which the schizophrenic-to-be cannot satisfactorily live.

The problem today is not one of hebephrenia. A minimum of schizophrenics today deteriorate in the old hebephrenic way—and then only if we provide the hospital conditions for it. The problem instead lies in what has been called ambulatory or pseudo-neurotic schizophrenia and what I call petit-mal schizophrenia—that is, the vast numbers of "disguised" people who have a small split between their cognition and emotion, who have the characteristic ambivalence about the choices open to them, who have a reduced and bizarre affect, but who rarely get to a psychiatrist or to a hospital. But the schizophrenic problem is still there in every sense of the word; it inhibits life in the same characteristic way and cries out for a solution with merely less flamboyance. The solution is first sought in a new marriage, a change of employment, travel, homosexuality, drugs, and in a hundred similar ways. The effect is to dull the total participation of the person in anything meaningful in life and to maintain withdrawal as a reserve. If such a person does get involved, he finds himself faltering at the critical moment of intimacy and may break down overtly. Most psychotherapy of marital dissidents reveals some flaw of this kind. On such a broad base, schizophrenia can no longer be considered an esoteric dis-ease—and we do not believe that saying the culture is schizophrenic solves the problem—but must instead be seen in its life-style or more normative aspects. Where this can be done, the prognosis for the patient is improved. This does not, however, by any means imply that hospital support, psychiatric maintenance, and fundamental medication have no place in the treatment of schizophrenia.

We might summarize all this by saying capsularly that the schizophrenic defensively develops a non–socially useful ego. He makes himself unloved and unlovable, except by his own ego, and he becomes the object of his own hatred as well. The unconscious part of him becomes the greatest priority of his life, and joys and sorrows are principally experienced there. If paranoid, he is yet able to say "j'accuse" to society, and to demand that society return what is his to him. But even paranoia no longer works for him in the long run. In place of Freud's concept of an "unbearable idea" as the basis of the neurotic reaction, we would say that an unbearable nuclear and distal metapsychological milieu is the basis of schizophrenia. Instead of the energy and libido model of the neurosis, the social and idealistic organization of self becomes the leading concept in understanding and interpreting schizophrenia. How that organization becomes disorganization is the question to which we address ourselves in this essay.

It is in the same vein that Binswanger talks about the *extravagant ideal* in schizophrenia, and an *inconsistency* and *disparateness* in their lives, which gives it that alogical quality. These patients are furthermore unable to "let be," to discontinue their search and preoccupation with the problem, and to solve it finally and permanently. This is uniquely different from anything the neurotic does. The neurotic, for all his obsession with mental health, has one eye peeled on the outside world and what gratification it can offer him. The schizophrenic, on the other hand, sets up the intrapsychic *in competition* with the interpersonal, and the latter slowly but surely loses out to his inner man. We may say that the secondary gains become life-exorbitant for the schizophrenic, but the neurotic secretly enjoys his. Schizophrenia is the only disease of record which does not cure itself, and its essential aspects as seen by the patient are magic, morals, and ideals rather than bacteria or proteins. Only its peculiar form of self-punishment frees it from its paradoxes, and it absolutizes itself by such forms, for after a certain point there is no self-return. Don Quixote finds it impossible then to be Sancho Panza. Life is lived as a metaphor. The schizophrenic lowers the level of life in order to preserve it. Above all, the schizophrenic takes the suffering upon himself and releases his family and society from obligation. This is directly contrary to the criminal who makes society suffer for its shortcomings.

II. LIFE-STYLE MODES

No one of record has been able to see the establishment of a life style from infancy to adulthood. Life styles are customarily sampled on a cross-sectional basis, and inferences made from the observations as to the interpersonal dynamics which produced such styles. This is obviously an unsatisfactory way to scientifically establish how people go about constructing their personality. It is one of the difficulties in understanding just what happens to a child who finally ends up with what we call schizophrenia. Be that as it may, the attempt to reconstruct the formative influences of the particular life style associated with schizophrenia must continue until such time as we can observe it in actual life.

On the basis of the schizophrenic phenomenology, we have drawn a number of inductive examples as to how this particular style of living or mode of being might have come into existence. Obviously, the ten functions which follow account for only a part of the social genesis, but they do serve to make more comprehensible the function schizophrenia serves in the personal autonomy of certain people. These functions are:

1. Taking-In and Giving-Out
2. Dread-ness
3. Despair
4. Greed
5. Shame
6. Magic
7. Creation
8. Insistence
9. Social Presentation
10. Temporality and Spatiality

1. *Taking-In and Giving-Out*

Sigmund Freud's description of the character aspects of the oral and the anal and phallic functions is a classic in psychopathology which has yet to be equaled. But he made little or no application of these formulations to schizophrenia, and few of his disciples have dared to do so. Invariably, schizophrenic patients have problems with food intake and food expulsion. But such problems are vastly different from the anorexia of the hysteric or the ulceration of the colitic. It is a surprising finding that psychosomatizing cannot serve the schizophrenic as a defense against anxiety as it does for the neurotic. If it could, we perhaps might not have the problem of schizophrenia in its present form. The body problems of the schizophrenic, on the other hand, are those of no-body, or a body that has lost energetic integration of organs and is therefore open to the wildest distortion and delusion. Such body symptoms do not so much provide pain to the patient as they do puzzlement and fear. A patient says half of her head is missing—which it is not—but she does not say she has a headache or that it hurts. The missing half-head is only symbolically missing, but the head nevertheless feels as if it is only half-way in its functioning.

The digestive system is peculiarly arranged so that it analogically mirrors the total life processes of the person. The super-consciousness of food intake, and of food outgo, is a form of special consciousness of the state of the ego. This is seen most cogently in Binswanger's "Case of Ellen West," where ravenous, devouring hunger, with a coordinate increase in body weight, was explicitly correlated with the psychotic intervention. And an ethereal, sylph-like shape, a body freedom from food, indicated social and perceptual organization and life meaning. Food for Ellen West then became the watchword by which she literally lived and died.

A patient of ours, Mavis Roberts, slim and attractive, stands in front of the mirror and actually sees herself as obese—a residual of adolescence, when she was grossly overweight and suffered a mortification of the body. Another patient says to us, "All I need in life is a good shit." By this he means that if he can only get rid of the waste he can be like other people.

We have noted that schizophrenics do not seem to wet the bed, as other problem children do. This seems to be reserved for the neurotic-to-be and the character-problem child, but they do have strange periods of diarrhea or constipation or both. And we have never seen a schizophrenic patient who doesn't have a history of either constipation or diarrhea. We were able to trace such bowel problems through three generations of one patient and found that all used the same toilet and had identical toilet rituals. Our guess is that the child-to-be-schizophrenic perhaps gets more laxatives than other children and gets greater attention to the anus and to anal expulsion than other children. One such mother we know regularly warmed the toilet seat for her child by first sitting on it.

The usual difficulties of feeding and voiding do not, of course, add up to schizophrenia. There is, rather, in some mothers an inconsistency in orality and anality which never permits complete acceptance of the mouth or anus by the child. The timing of oral and anal mastery is also thereby upset so that the natural maturational hierarchy of impulses and control never actualizes itself. Mothers of schizophrenics are notably unsure about feeding and defecating, which is why they so often bring fruit to their sons and daughters in the mental hospital. Eating then assumes a confused, if not dangerous, quality and makes the schizophrenic a fertile soil for bizarre digestive problems. Here also is the possibility of paranoia, of poisoning, or of the magic nuturing apple of Madame Sechehaye's Renee. Putting the body image back together in psychotherapy restores the pristine and involuntary functions of eating, digesting, and eliminating without bizarre obsession. Kent, in speaking of the body, correctly says:

> During therapy, the patient's impressions are that changes take place in the direction of increased symmetry [of body function] and they feel that forces which produce a balancing effect have been brought into play.[32]

Becoming pregnant produces changes in the body conformation and in the body image. This is in the direction of being fat. Most women are ashamed of, or resentful of, the loss of attractiveness and nubility in pregnancy, but still others find relief in it. In the schizophrenic, pregnancy is intolerable for these reasons, but they also have the counter-need to create. They would like a child by immaculate conception and without pregnancy. Finally, the creative need is set up against the body self in almost impossible conflict.

Tactuality and olfaction are relatively unexplored aspects of behavioral science. For the schizophrenic they play a greater part in reality orientation than for others, and they necessarily come into the therapy as well. Mavis Roberts regularly touched her inner vaginal labia, and then smelled her hands, to reassure herself that she was a viable female. The odor of feces as well is particularly attractive to these patients, who scrutinize each bowel movement, and olfactory delusions are perhaps more common in schizophrenics than in any other kind of psychopathology. And schizophrenics seem at times to smell the therapeutic climate rather than feel it. The smell and textual quality of food are to them as important as the gustation.

It must be apparent that such a child grows up with an over-concern about his body, about his nourishment, and about his urination and defecation. Quite often the parents themselves have had allergies, food problems, gastrointestinal ulcerations, and the like, and become sensitized in this way. Personal growth then becomes more evaluated by one's inner environment or internal processes than by interpersonal successes. A special consciousness of the inner world develops as a displacement of the burgeoning social world, so that the normal pleasures of food and the survival function of eating become a curious and bizarre property of mental conflict.

2. *Dread-ness*

Dread is a concept which Kierkegaard[33] brought to philosophic respectability and Sartre[34] applied more directly to the problems of life and behavior. In psychopathology, dread needs to be distinguished from anxiety on the one hand and fear on the other. It appears to us that what is crucial in the development of schizophrenia is dread and not anxiety, although the two concepts are almost inextricably intertwined.

Dread is the subjective and symbolic statement of fear, and anxiety is its phenomenological manifestation. Dread is more long-range, more encompassing, and less situational than fear. Dread is in a sense the fear of fear. Here is what Ellen West had to say about her dread:

> This is the horrible part of my life: it is filled with dread. Dread of eating, dread of hunger, dread of the dread. Only death can save me from this dread. Every day is like walking on a dizzying ridge, an eternal balancing on cliffs. It is useless to have analysis tell me that I want precisely this dread, this tension. It sounds brilliant, but it does not help my aching heart. Who wants this tension, who, what? I see nothing any more, everything is blurred, all the threads are tangled.[35]

The dread of the chronic alcoholic is seen in every sign or symbol of a cocktail bar, a liquor store, and even a liquor bottle. The homosexual finds dread in every sexually attractive man, in the cop on the vice beat, and in women who challenge his erotic situation. But in essence there are only two basic dreads: the dread of self and the dread of death. It is the self one dreads most, for the self can at times take over cognition, perception, and feeling, and put obsession, anxiety, and compulsion in their place. The normal symbols of food, drink, sexuality, and similar others become transmuted into dangers, with fear and anxiety as their accompaniment. Dread becomes pervasive and the personality finally attempts to dissociate the self from it-self. All behavior then becomes the escape from dread.

The basic dread is that of dying. This is man's chief repression. Whether Eros is in a constant dialogue with Thanatos, as Freud believed, is an open question; but no man lives without that great question of finality which hangs over him. The appearance of institutional religion was purposely designed to help him with this problem. Dread may be considered the imbalance between the id, the ego, and the superego—that is, between the creative forces and the extinction of that creativity. Eros and Thanatos, by their intercurrent power, shift the polarity of that balance and the closer one comes to the appreciation of death, the greater the dread.

There is also a form of dread which accompanies getting what one wants—of becoming what one wants to be. Dread and hope stand in a special relationship to each other, and hope reduces dread. When the object of that hope is gained, and when that hope goes counter to the superego, a sense of dread as well as guilt may prevail. This is specifically the case in schizophrenia where the patient fights the satisfaction of needs and seems everlastingly to reduce all hope to nothingness. Joy opposes dread; but some people have to set limits on their joy or an even greater dread will supervene.

Paranoia is dread run riot, a claiming of any and all persons (and things) for its dread. This in part accounts for the frequent frenzy of the paranoid and his latent ability to diminish and destroy. It is necessary for the paranoid to displace the dread of self away from his personal responsibility and onto others.

The mothering persons of schizophrenics are dread-ful people. They have a hidden dread of themselves, fear Eros and Thanatos, are cynical of men and their society, but displace this dread and convert it by reaction formation to the service of humanity, employing their designated child for this purpose. They insist that this child do something about their dread, make the family happier, and improve the lot of the world. They present themselves publicly as dread-free and socially capable at the same time that they communicate anxiety and dread in a hundred hidden ways. The difficulty of family therapy is that the dread becomes a more conscious one and can destroy the family if not properly handled.

3. *Despair*

The summative function of dread is despair. Despair finds only a closed circle, with no way to freedom possible. It seeks a way out; and not finding it, suicide, self-castration, and starvation are possible. The future seems an impossibility and only an unusual act of some kind can open it. Despair such as this leads to depression, which is the act of punishment for the despair, but also for the possibilities of its resolution. Despair comes in waves and employs obsessional ideation as its functional structure. It is temporarily relieved by the closeness of others and by a dependence on them, but despair can find only its own conclusion and not the conclusion of others.

Despair is regularly a part of schizophrenia. The despair involves the proven impossibility of attaining the Extravagant Ideal, the self-reflection of the deep retreat into the self, and, finally, the ultimate sequestration by society as undesirables. Nothing matters! But this form of despair, in order to preserve existence at all, must be turned into a form of curious, even joyous, indifference. When this happens, the full flowering of the schizophrenic life style is then considered in bloom.

There is evidence that the family field from which the schizophrenic comes is one of despair. But it is not an acknowledged despair, for often the family seems happy. As with dread, the despair is finally deposited in the self of one of its designated members. The family can thereby deny its despair and enhance its meaning and purpose by dedicating itself to changing the despair in the sick one. All this becomes unmasked in family therapy, where the family despair can be rightly apportioned among the members who have earned it.

4. *Greed*

The schizophrenic patient is particularly prone to greediness. But this is not the greed we use in everyday parlance; rather, it is an existential greed that arrogates to itself the fate of mankind. Everything is overdone, and even then done with a vengeance. The greediness involves the search for beauty, for freedom and justice, and for total personal expression. Whatever the schizophrenic does, he must do at his apogee. He cannot be satisfied with less. Eating is gluttony or it is starvation; sex is continuous or it is absent for months, etc. This gives the drives of the patient a peculiar waxing and waning quality, an over- and under-determination, which sets them apart from normal drives, and the satiation of the drive seems to come more rapidly than for others. At times the greediness seems to be an over-compensation for the patient's actual deprivation; but it is actually more relevant to the ideals and social interest of the patient than to his frustration.

As reported earlier, Binswanger has particularly noted the Extravagant Ideal in the schizophrenic. Most of us are content with a certain quality and quantity of life; we reconcile ourselves to the paradoxes and absurdities in it, and do not set our star toward the paradise archetype. But the schizophrenic cannot reduce his social greediness; he cannot compromise with the social fictions and paradoxes extant; and we have come to believe that after a certain time he does not want to. Mavis Roberts felt intense hostility toward a four-month-old infant she saw being cuddled. She herself wanted all of the cuddling available in the world. And this is the way it is with most such patients.

Existential greed sweeps all things before it, but it is not a voluntary thing. It is a mission to "save the world" rather than narcissism, like some of the proselytizing evangelical sects, and in this way also to save oneself. The purpose is to remove paradox and Absurdity and have a truly joyous world given over to love. The schizophrenic considers everyone in bad faith, whereas he is in good faith. He cannot understand how Everyman can live with the Absurd and paradoxy and still find life worth living. He has somehow missed the wonderful resilience of the human being, who while recognizing the limitations of social existence can still ride with the tides without seriously deviating from his life style in a more or less permanent and unrelieved dissent.

Of course, the mothering person demonstrates the same kind of rigidity and greed. We have been impressed, in the family therapy of schizophrenics, by the extent to which the mother takes over and controls the family, and how limited her own existence is because of the takeover. She can live everyone's life but her own. As her children grow, she is more than ever determined to make something of them, to unconsciously live through them even more fully; and should this be unmasked, she collapses like a house of cards. In one sense the entire family is a product of existential greed.

5. *Shame*

Shame is a function of the ego and, of course, the superego. To feel appropriately ashamed is what every child is supposed to learn in his development. Of course, each culture and subculture experiences shame in a different way. The shameful things, the Judeo-Christian sins, carry varied loadings and are often disregarded, but they lodge in the psyche like permanent deposits and produce their guilt. The man without shame is a psychopath.

Original sin, that basic postulate of Christianity, makes us all sinners at birth, but offers redemption in a variety of easy ways. One has only to have faith in the godhead and to confess to his vicar. We have often wondered why the clergy were so reluctant to bring personal salvation to the schizophrenic as compared to other patients, for we saw little of it in more than 15 years of service in the mental hospital. Being mentally ill is not a sin because it is involuntary, like having tuberculosis, and there is nothing to be redeemed. But what if schizophrenia turned out to be a life style rather than a helpless illness—would it then be open to sinfulness? Parents do feel ashamed of their schizophrenic children. Being autistic in this way could be a sin against community, a nonparticipation in Christian brotherhood, and the schizophrenic damned because he did not fit it with the absolution afforded.

Schizophrenics as adolescents feel great shame; even as adults they are full of concealed amounts of it. But the shame of the schizophrenic is different from our shame and we cannot easily empathize with him. The schizophrenic does not see himself as a sinner at all, even though he has eaten of the forbidden existential fruit from the tree of knowledge. He feels beyond Christian shame, but deeply into existential shame. The wars fought under religious auspices— say, the Crusades—have always been crueler than territorial wars, and the power wrested by war and then abused—say, by men like Heinrich Himmler—has invariably been by men of an early devout religious background. Schizophrenia is in a sense an antireligious religion in that it opts for peace, brotherhood, and fulfillment for man but seeks it in man himself rather than in a godhead.

The schizophrenic's personal history reveals that in the most subtle of ways he has been vastly shamed by his mother (as well as loved), and it is interesting that he in turn becomes the greatest source of shame to her. A part of the psychotherapeutic task is to bring this earliest recollection of shame back to him, but in a new and different framework. We must refuse his exemption from shame while at the same time evolving with him its more human aspects. True shame is always social.

6. *Magic*

Mavis Roberts wore a "sun-moon" amulet to each session without fail; she was never without it. One day we asked her if we could hold it for a few moments. With great reluctance she removed it from her neck and tendered it. From here we progressed to the point where she would allow us to keep it overnight, then for a week, and finally for an entire month. Now she no longer wears it at all except in moments of regression.

All schizophrenics at some time or other believe themselves to be witches and warlocks and practice a magic in their rituals and obsessions. This is the magic of the unconscious. The history of psychiatry has also been identified with witch doctors, shamans, and the like, who practiced magical rites. Mavis made the first slight change in her schizophrenic life style when I challenged her to cast a spell over me, and later when I placed my "magic" power against hers and bested her.

The current popular interest in astrology, ESP, clairvoyance, and allied phenomena is an indication of the pull such superordinate phenomena have on all people. They represent, in a way, a failure of Western science to answer the deepest problems people have. C. G. Jung was convinced that the scientific postulate of causality was overly simplistic to explain the wide behavioral phenomena we all experience. He therefore derived the principle of synchronicity. The narrow borderland between established religious practice and occult phenomena, between the output of saintly poetic mystics and scientific ordinators of the future, etc., is an uncomfortable one. More than we consciously recognize, such concepts as luck, fate, chance, good fortune, god, etc., are regularly incanted over that of probability values by scientists themselves. Magic is superordinate transformation.

In schizophrenia, magic protects and brings possible change where none seems feasible. The patient leaves the world of logic, causality, and reasoning for a broader-based experience, and he finds a greater comfort and security in it, albeit an estrangement. In this new world he can limit paradoxy and reduce Absurdity. He responds like the person who is having his first awesome LSD trip, and he wants to retain the perceptual world he finds there after the trip is over. Not only that; he now feels he has the power to alchemically convert paradox into authenticity and to make it better for all. Like the hipster who, in response to hostility, says "love" or "peace," the patient's message is clarity and joy. From perhaps the most powerless of social persons he becomes in himself the most powerful.

The dangers of living in everlasting magic are great, for the world of reality, as we well know, is not that satisfactory. All of us hunger for the womb, for the eternal return, for the paradise arche-type. The magician-schizophrenic becomes a primary symbolist; he finds magic in food, sex, and people and refuses to yield to the de-mands of reality. He then lives like Merlin, but in a milieu unim-pressed with his powers.

The psychotherapy of schizophrenia does not call for meeting such magic head on, but must first demonstrate a basic sympathy with it. Later, it is necessary to show the patient how the uncon-scious is as lawful as the conscious, that it is not magic at all, and that universal causality carries an important social payoff. He must come to understand that a power which cannot be shared socially with others is actually an impotency. If this were not true, why then should the psychotherapist also not use magic in his cure? (Of course, some think we do!)

We accept the possibility that mothering persons of schizophren-ics dabble in magic as well. They inculcate in their designated offspring a sensitivity to the uncanny and the magical. They them-selves solve things in magical and fantastic ways, particularly when reality becomes badly blocked for them. The child learns that relief is to be found in this way and is subtly encouraged in it by his mother. Later he finds Blake, Buddha, Guerdjieff, Nietzsche, St. John of the Cross, and many others, who supply him with a poetical/religious dimension backed by peer-group support. As an adult he becomes a labeled carrier of the mystical tradition, but in a psychiatric phrasing he becomes the bearer of the primary process of the unconscious.

7. *Creation*

Schizophrenics are poets in disguise. They are of the surrealist su-premacy, whose art society refuses to accept. They are the masters of the symbol and metaphor, and they hold the figurative key to life. They very often have the deepest insights into the human con-dition which come to others with only the greatest difficulty or nev-er at all. All books written by recovered schizophrenics, as, for ex-ample, *I Never Promised You a Rose Garden,* reveal a poignant quality that almost constitutes the rebirth of a crucified suffering. Schizophrenics somehow need to be involved with the beginnings and ends of things, and are constantly preoccupied with how man elects things. It is therefore difficult to see how any psychotherapy of schizophrenia can proceed without the use of painting, sculpture, creative writing, or similar modes. By his art, the schizophrenic attempts surrealistically to reconstruct his world, using a new logic and reality to do it. He is continually creating and recreating, and does the same with his psychotherapy.

The schizophrenic is preoccupied with the myth of his eternal return. This is not Karma in the Hindu sense or its religious equivalent. Not knowing who he is, he believes he has had or will have some other life somewhere. This "other" life calls for the highest degree of purposiveness, and his mission is to save society from its own paradoxes and Absurdities. But no one listens and his new forms bring laughter and cynicism. He is finally driven to the outer margins of reality and becomes more bizarre than communicative.

In an earlier book on general psychotherapy, we have hypothesized the nature of the therapeutic hour as consisting of an *opening* or *platform* statement, an *incubation,* a *development,* a *closing,* and an *acting upon*.[36] Any single therapeutic hour, we said, may be made up of one or a hundred of such therapeutic sequential monads. Insight, growth, and development flow out of these successive intellectual structures, backed in every instance by correlated affect. In the case of the schizophrenic patient, however, there is still an additional interview function which we call the *archetypal statement,* a final stage of insight, and which we did not describe earlier.

The archetypal statement is a relatively late formulation by the patient which requires no interpretation whatsoever and, indeed, just is. It is an aphoristically arrived-at truth of considerable brilliance and synthesizes important aspects of the patient's thought and behavior. It comes spontaneously, almost unpredictably, but requires considerable incubation and working through. Normal insight is pedestrian to it. Its appearance in treatment is a harbinger of better things to come, and a leap into growth invariably follows. The following archetypal statements were all given by our various schizophrenic patients.

1. The precariousness of life hasn't been allowed into my purview.
2. For once I was screwing and my vagina wasn't doing it alone.
3. That eight pounds of flesh was my defense against body fulfillment.
4. Magic imprisons me by its rituals.
5. You are taking my impotence away.
6. Appetite is for me a dirty word.
7. I feel like Atlas shouldering the load of myself.
8. Last night for once I didn't feel fucked but loved.
9. As soon as my man has an existence, I have none at all.
10. I don't want to fuck to the piper anymore.

These archetypal statements are a part of the creative effort of the schizophrenic to deepen his way of being and to communicate it in a more socialized form. They lead ultimately to a revision in the way of handling paradoxes and Absurdities and to a more real and socialized person. Their presence in treatment is a most encouraging sign and they represent creativity at work in the patient.

8. *Insistence*

There is an aspect of the life style of schizophrenics which I call *Insistence*. It is a self-rigidity and self-demand which leaves the patient quite unable to vary his behavior in necessary situations and even to tolerate it in others. He tends to take people and objectives over; he insists on having his way; and, when people demur, he is more surprised and chagrined than angry. This is often seen in his psychotherapy, where no model of existence, no transference, no countertransference, no love, no logic—nothing—can move the patient. This is not a cognitive matter but one of a biased ego and constitutes his strength as well as his weakness.

It was the same with his mother, who in family therapy reveals an intransigence and severity of purpose one finds only in fundamentalist religionists or in powerful corporate executives. It is also related to the breakthrough discovery of the scientist, where a highly original but irrational solution is at first resisted by all—the greater the resistance, the more the discoverer believes he is right.

If treatment is to be successful, it is necessary to change this Insistence factor in the patient, for he cannot survive socially with it. Most often the change comes about through the humanistic and weathering influence of the psychotherapy itself, but there are usually times when a terrible confrontation with the patient is necessary to change it. The denouement may then make or break the entire treatment. It is the quality of Insistence, we should note, which permits the schizophrenic to see his treatment through, as well as the difficult life he has made for himself, and it is not intended to make a docile person of him. However, *Insistence* is a sign of a nonsocially useful ego and must to some extent be tempered by the amenities of social life. In plaintive moments the patient even verbalizes this.

9. *Social Presentation*

The appearance, dress, and grooming of the schizophrenic is always somewhat quixotic. Even if the raiment is of superior quality, which at least in private practice it most often is, the way it is worn leaves something to be desired. There is a loss of chic and fashion, even in patients who have been reared in it, and the wearer obviously loses something in its wearing. It is not that the schizophrenic is slovenly, but there is instead an indifference to the niceties of good grooming, which might place him in the vanguard socially and attract people.

We have matched this disability up with their mothers—the fathers are certainly different—and have rarely found a well-turned-out mother of a hospitalized schizophrenic patient. It takes a studied effort, and a certain open and flirtatious life style, to be chic, to be perfectly groomed, and to feel this as a part of one's ego. The grooming casualness of the hipster is also an attempt to avoid acculturation, but his lack of grooming has order and meaning in it, which the schizophrenic's does not. Psychotherapy slowly changes this, and improved dress, grooming, etc., are often the first sign of growth. We watch for these things, eagerly acknowledge them, and promote them in every way. Interestingly enough, we feel ourselves beginning to be socially attracted to the patient because of his altered social presentation, and we know we are on the right track in his treatment.

10. *Temporality and Spatiality*

Heidegger and his followers cogently revealed that time and space have personal meaning beyond their physical properties. They may even eventually turn out to be the core of the neurosis. It is certainly true that one sees the most elaborate distortions in temporality and spatiality in schizophrenics. To be able to live in our time, and in our space, is the best single sign of the acceptance of one's culture. Ellen West both encapsulated and dilated time, expanded and contracted her life space, and lived perpetually in a dread-ful world that would not retain its physical boundaries. The self refers itself to space and time for orientation. If these givens lack normalization, a bizarre effect is introduced in experience.

The present moment, the past, the becoming future—one's size and shape, the contours, constancy, and reachability of the perceptual world, etc.—all become porous. Finally, time and space may be largely given up, as is done in the catatonic and hebephrenic. Compare, for example, the meaning of 50 minutes to a psychoanalyst and to a hospitalized schizophrenic patient. For the former, 50 minutes is an inviolate premise, provides for the transition from one patient to the next, and relates basically to the production of his income. For the latter, 50 minutes is like 10 or 100 minutes, and has no social, work, or creative meaning at all. Such concepts as "nothing," "forever," "never," etc., mean more to him than 50 minutes.

But time and space hang heavy upon the schizophrenic person and he cannot escape them completely. They form the foundation of his social disorganization; but his human need is to be organized, and this means time and space as we normally use them.

We believe that one begins in this area by insisting upon the regularity of appointments, their temporal and spatial meaning, and their structure in relationship to other structures. From here one goes to the time and space of other people, and then back to the patient. The schizophrenic never really becomes a fully organized person attending religiously to time and space, in part because his earliest milieu never proposed it as a basic proposition of existence, or he resists, instead, precisely that.

III. THE PSYCHOTHERAPY

The psychotherapy of schizophrenia is not a uniform thing. The techniques of Rosen, Sullivan, Arieti, Searles, Binswanger, Jackson, Wynne, Spotnitz, and others reveal profound differences in conception and execution. One approach may be supremely directive; another may follow the more passive classical analytic style; still a third may give up the dyad entirely and focus on the family. Be that as it may, there is still a core or commonality in all psychic treatment of the schizophrenic and that core may be the healer himself.

Why does the psychotherapist select the most difficult patients of all to work with? And in doing so he goes somewhat against the tides of his profession, and he gives up more than other psychotherapists in order to treat them. There is a seriousness of purpose, a dedication, in the psychotherapy of schizophrenia which is unique to the annals of psychotherapy. Jackson offers us a clue in the following quotation:

> That is why I tell myself, and I think it is partly true, that I like to think I can turn it off and on at will, just as the actor knows that the play comes to an end in an hour. But what I suspect is that I also do it because I can't help it, and because I can't stand incorporation of the patient's feelings, and I somehow look as though I am controlling it by pretense, like bluffing.[37]

In a sense, one does not treat schizophrenia; rather, one lives it. The vicissitudes of bringing growth and change to a schizophrenic constitute a highly involved and personal process whose fundaments lie deeply buried in the existence of both participants. Such psychotherapy cannot be done with the objectivity one would like to have. And to attempt objectivity with a reluctant schizophrenic patient is to defeat the therapy before it begins. One must therefore inquire why it is that some of us find certain rewards in this ungracious form of treatment.

There is of course no precise answer, and even the psychotherapists of schizophrenia themselves seem at a loss to explain it. We would venture three depthful hypotheses, realizing that they are by no means the entire story. The first is that the psychotherapist finds the metaphorical answer to the riddle of life lodged in them and, as a corollary, therapists need to be present at the birthplace of creative existence. The second hypothesis is that there is something residual in the family background of the psychotherapist himself— some unfinished business—which ties him closer to the schizophrenic (and his family) than other psychotherapists. He has been left charged with an unconscious mission to bring peace and serenity to his own family, to other families, and then to the most disturbed of all, the schizophrenic. The psychotherapist of schizophrenia is in a way the Don Quixote of psychiatry.

The third hypothesis is fear. The psychotherapist of schizophrenia is less afraid of his unconscious, his demons, and has a greater readiness to tackle the same in others. Indeed, he has a form of thrust in this direction. The possibility of becoming psychotic in treating chronic schizophrenia is not a matter of fantasy, and all of us have had suicidal and homicidal impulses aroused in us. The dangers with a hysteric are easily much less. We are all painfully aware of how tenuously reality is held in us, of the gross temptations of the id, and of the Svengali of regression constantly standing in the wings. We do not usually allow patients to regularly challenge the deepest parameters in us, and we consciously or unconsciously give the patient up rather than face such travail. But the psychotherapy of schizophrenia precisely calls for this as a regular thing if it is to succeed. It is no happenstance that there is a "burning out" process in regularly working with chronic schizophrenia and that the field is littered with defectors and suicides.[38] Regardless of the method used, such a psychotherapist is a person who has come more to terms with his unconscious, has perhaps suffered more than his due, and is less afraid to face the ultimate verities and denigrations of existence. Indeed, he finds unique satisfactions and beauty in the miserable process! According to Malone,

> The kind of person who psychologically treats schizophrenia is apt to be the kind of person who has available the kind of feelings that are apt to make the patient accept these feelings as being true; second, the intensity of the patient's need for such feelings and the juxtaposition of these two things create the phenomena we are talking about.[30]

Psychotherapists of schizophrenia have even been at times considered schizoid or schizophrenic.[40] While we do not go this far, as we have said before, they are closer to the demonic in themselves, they are more attuned to the symbol and metamessage, and they need more than others to get to that molten center which represents the birthplace of the self. These patients have a kind of beauty, unmatched by neurotics or others, and the narcissism they demonstrate is more existential than selfish. Such a patient can literally destroy you, but it would be for love rather than hate. The treatment process with them unfolds with the character and disorder of a well-written book if, of course, a master author is at work.

To describe our way of treating schizophrenia, we want to set the stage by quotations from Ludwig Binswanger and Alfred Adler. Binswanger writes:

> What we call psychotherapy is basically no more than an attempt to bring the patient to a point where he can "see" the manner in which the totality of human existence or "being-in-the-world" is structured and to see at which of its junctures he has overreached himself. That is: the goal of psychotherapy is to bring the patient safely back "down to earth" from his extravagances. Only from this point is any new *departure* and ascent possible.[41]

Kurt Adler, speaking for his father, says:

> It is only logical therefore that Adler's main weapon in combatting the schizophrenic's style of life was encouragement, and

he states that to cure schizophrenia, first of all, the physician must be more hopeful than the patient, Second, the therapist must become the first meaningful relationship that the patient ever had, by use of the kindliest and friendliest approach and by unfailing, constant cooperation and obvious interest in the patient and his welfare. At the same time, the therapist must be constantly aware of the patient's exaggerated sensitivity to even the slightest hints of humiliation. The approach has to be continued until the patient becomes convinced that fruitful cooperation with another human being is possible, until he becomes more hopeful as to the achievement of some of his goals, and until he learns to feel less isolated, and more like a fellow human being.[42]

The *tour de force* in the treatment of schizophrenia is to get the patient involved in the treatment at all. Like the alcoholic, the schizophrenic is wary of the psychotherapist and interprets him as an inauthentic person. He is also afraid he will die in the process. His medical history is such that he has constantly been misunderstood by healers, essentially rejected by them, and even made to suffer more, all in the name of humanitarian science. Is it any wonder that he quickly rejects our offer of help? Medicine is traditionally a doing-to process, and the schizophrenic fears anything done to him. More than any other patient of record, he disbelieves that we have something better to offer him. In addition, from the phenomenological point of view, he has solved the many paradoxes and Absurdities of social life and he therefore demands proof that the therapist has at least gone this far in his own life. This is the basic dilemma of the psychotherapy of schizophrenia.

How much are we willing to acknowledge the basic corruption and paradoxes of culture to him at the same time that we psychotherapists are some of the prime benefactors of its institutions? The strain of what we are, our being, as against what the schizophrenic refuses to become, takes its toll of us in treating him. Of course, we can shout him down, as in direct analysis; uneasily confront him against his family, as in family therapy; outnumber him, as in multiple therapy; or out-analyze him, as in psychoanalysis of schizophrenia. All of these are, alas, merely hedges against the mainstream of the necessary and sufficient encounter which is necessary to tackle schizophrenia.

On a practical level, the difficulties are not so rarefied and impossible if certain conditions are met. What must be practically accomplished are the following:

1. The patient has to be given some newer concept of himself as an acceptable part of the Absurd world.
2. The patient has to be given back the right to live.
3. The patient must rediscover his body.
4. The patient must develop an increasing tolerance of paradox and incorporate it into his personal existence in more viable forms.
5. The patient must learn to give up some of his symbols and magic for molar acts which have a new social meaning for him.
6. The patient must rediscover a new life style not necessarily approved or disapproved by his mother or proximal or distal family.

To attain these things requires not only a special technical stance but certain modeling properties as well. No one should be fooled into believing that love, friendship, or good will alone can help schizophrenics. The psychotherapist must be like a chess master in his handling of the transference, countertransference, identification, counteridentification, introjection, insight, and a form of real friendship as well. The sensitivity of the psychotherapy is so great that peremptory discontinuance of the relationship by one or the other is an ever-present loaded jack-in-the-box, and the death of the patient or the worsening of his condition, as an ultimate possibility, is not to be ruled out. For this reason, no such patient should be treated unless one feels the strongest pull to be with that particular patient. Such psychotherapy also has all the earmarks of temporary marriage; and a real marriage, I must say, is sometimes easier to get out of than the temporary marriage with a schizophrenic patient.

Technically, the therapy of schizophrenia employs a wider repertory of therapist behavior than any other psychotherapy. One must be passive, silent, uncommunicative, and loving, but also dynamic, active, talkative, symbolizing, and aggressing. The bodies of the two participants are both closer together and further apart. There is conventional interpretation and insight-formation, but mostly there is a living or experiencing-together process of the greatest moment. The transference and its analysis are not so central, but the contemporary relationship is. The future as well comes in for greater utilization. The interaction requires a vehicle, an apparatus on which to hang the hat of the cure, and if we want to call this transference, so be it. But what this vehicle is is of secondary importance, although in the earlier periods of therapy it provides a necessary security for the psychotherapist.

Scheflen describes the various therapeutic behaviors he found in direct analysis. They apply here as well.

1. Promising and rewarding
2. Threatening and punishing
3. Suggesting and instructing
4. Coercing
5. Rendering service
6. Using group pressure
7. Ridiculing, shaming, discrediting
8. Appealing and challenging
9. Interrupting and diverting
10. Offering a more acceptable alternative
11. Misrepresenting
12. Imitating and caricaturing
13. Playing certain roles
14. Permitting the patient to act out
15. Reassurance
16. Direct confronting and interpreting[43]

The rule in our work is that whatever pushes the treatment edge forward is to be used, and what constitutes the dialogue of the moment depends upon the feeling and intention of the psychotherapist —and the patient's response to it. But the ability to set limits, to be silent, to be angry, and to confine the mentation stream or interaction to smaller bursts of energy is equally important. If permitted, the schizophrenic will run away with the game ball, or perhaps merely refuse to play. One has to be a referee, as well as a player on both sides. As is also well known, the patient will severely test the patience, endurance, and love and hate of the therapist almost beyond belief.

It is best to follow the patient's lead—to deal with what he brings each time—or to be silent if he is silent. In this form of treatment the nonverbal counts more heavily—at least in the beginning—so that careful attention must be given to postural, facial, gestural, and other bodily cues. Invariably the crises come, and the patient is saying something by them. When this happens, we analyze ourselves carefully for mistakes or for new needs which have come up and which the crisis symbolically represents. Once having found the solution, we are not apt to give up the new position under the patient's anger and threats, but we phrase our noncompliance lovingly and rationally if we can. At times we soliloquize, using analogues to the present situation, and, where the previous crisis was successfully surmounted, we hit at that. We never role play. And while we don't play into the psychosis, we do stay with the patient all the way. We handle paranoia most often by disclaiming participation in the projections while acknowledging that we can understand how one would think that way. As to hallucinations and delusions of a more benign sort, we will sometimes gently hammer away at them, as not very useful or tenable in the life of the patient. We do this over and over again as they come up again and again.

Somatizing and delusions of the body become a later problem. One tries to ignore them at first, but they may have a physical reality. At any rate, "having half a head" or "one's heart being missing" or "being rotten inside" are metaphoric fears of an inability to be a body, to have a necessary body image. We respond to the hidden fear. These are times when touching the patient, along with the necessary verbal reassurance, helps a great deal. We also pride ourselves on our own bodies and use them as models. There is a danger here, however, that the patient may want your body rather than his own.

Whatever the content of the hour, we never lose hope and optimism that the patient will voluntarily change his life style. We point out again and again that he is on a self-defeating road, and that he is missing most of the pure delights of existence. We may even tell him that he is missing a lot of good sex, along with other beautiful things, and that he ought to shape up. In this connection some of the rational-emotive techniques of Albert Ellis[44] serve well. Again, all of this may be wrong if the timing is incorrect and the patient lacks the necessary security.

Money, sex, personal achievement, family congeniality, everything by which our culture lives, are taboo or disgusting to the patient. He brings all of them up with a negative phrasing, and they are all things which we psychotherapists have a great deal of. One listens to this without defense until the patient slowly admits that they might have their place.

Finally, one of these can be used more intensively, for analytic grist for the mill, and worked through. We pick the one the patient has the least choler about and can handle best. We then become directive and confronting, and even dare the patient not to see or feel it.

Nothing in this form of treatment militates against needed family therapy sessions, or the use of plastic arts for synthesizing images and feelings either in or outside of the hour. It is folly to believe that even four hours a week can do all the healing. The patient lives his therapy outside as well. This, of course, encourages the intrusion of the patient in our lives at odd hours, but one had better be prepared for it and learn to handle it. We have found painting and sculpting to be most useful for uncovering unconscious archetypes and for synthesizing things learned verbally in the psychotherapy itself. We have described some of these procedures elsewhere.[45]

Our belief is that every schizophrenic, in the earliest phases of treatment, should be considered a witch or warlock. And most patients bring their magic to their therapy. Schizophrenics are perpetually carrying amulets or magic symbols on them, and the process of psychotherapy is one of reducing the magic and replacing it by reality. We bring the therapy back again and again to the present reality, keep focusing on it, and sometimes dare the patient to use his magic on us. I repeat endlessly that he is a human being, as we are, and if there were magic ours would be stronger than his.

As the patient finds that his "secret" system is more and more attached, that his schizoid premises are slowly going by the board, he of course fights back. This is the most crucial time of the psychotherapy. If the psychotherapy is genuinely producing growth, the client will sometimes attempt an act of desperation to avoid the consequences of his new growth. This can be a suicidal attempt, an attempt to hurt or destroy the psychotherapist, an offer of sexual alliance, or a failure to return to treatment. The Either/Or being conflict is now in full swing and the way in which the psychotherapist handles this crisis makes or breaks the entire treatment.

Obviously, the psychotherapist does not want the patient to die, nor does he himself want to get hurt, and sexuality is out of the question with the patient if only of the certainty that no pleasure is to be found in it at the time. There are few rules to go by here, and the psychotherapist must not become frightened or panic. We are always comforted at such times by the knowledge that we have done our best, and we do not forget that it is the patient's choice what he does with himself, but we help him to be clear about it. And we give every support at this time, maintaining an almost superhuman patience and watchfulness and availability. As many hours as needed are given, and if necessary the psychotherapist goes to the patient. But we also make it clear that if the patient wants to die there is nothing we can do about it; yet it would cerainly be a loss to us and to society. We also make it clear that we will defend ourselves with any and all measures, even calling the sheriff if necessary. Slowly but definitely the patient stops to consider the alternatives in his life at the moment. His disturbance is a kind of proof to him that his life-philosophical position is not so secure as he once thought it was. He begins to doubt his autism, ambivalence, and delusions. There can really be no basic change in the schizophrenic situation without surmounting such upheavals, and any psychotherapy which does not have them is in our opinion suspect. The resistances to change seem to accumulate in schizophrenia into major active positions rather than presenting themselves uniformly over time, as in the neuroses.

In psychoanalysis the working through of the resistances in hysteria was the *gran via* to successful prosecution of the psychotherapy. In the neuroses the resistances come in orderly and predictable

fashion, and are at any rate related to the repressed nuclear conflict. They can be correlated with the feeling states which arise in
the psychotherapy, and with the ebb and flow of the growing edge.
This is not so true for the schizophrenic, where no consistent pathological design is visible insofar as the resistances to changing them
are concerned. The schizophrenic overreacts to stimuli that seem of
no great consequence at the moment, and he resists when the resistance itself does not seem the proper mode for the defense of the
self. It is at first a most startling and peculiar therapeutic thing; but
in some way the resistances add up to a totality, not only of a refusal of psychotherapy but a refusal of the social life as well. It is a
mistake to believe that every resistance has to be analyzed with
schizophrenics, or even that every concept the patient voices requires tracking to its source. One learns to pass a great deal over in
such psychotherapy and there is invariably a second chance given
us.

Resistance involves transference and countertransference. As we
know, Freud believed that schizophrenics were not capable of a
transference and, furthermore, that their resistances could not be
overcome. More than a half-century's experience has revealed this
to be not quite true. A transference is possible with schizophrenics,
but it is not the neurotic transference which Freud knew best. The
schizophrenic transference waxes and wanes in very strange ways
and is less dependable as the vehicle of growth or change. More important than the transference, however, is the identification and
counteridentification which develop as related or opposed to transference. Strangely enough, parents are not that important to the
schizophrenic's evolvement that the presence or absence of a transference means that psychotherapy can or cannot be done with
them. The identifications, introjections, and reality presence are
more important for resolving the frozen style of life.

The real problem of resistance is on the side of the psychotherapist who, after making a treatment commitment, develops disturbing
feelings and fears, perhaps a boredom, a feeling of a lifetime struggle, and wants out, or at least an abridgment of the vicissitudes he is
experiencing.

So much of the schizophrenic's therapeutic behavior is an intuitive reaction to the therapist's hidden feelings and impulses that wanting out on both sides becomes critical. The patient is then apt to get violent. This was indeed the way it was with his parents, and what forced him into a general retreat. The schizophrenic regularly monitors his intimate world for disaffection, paradox, lack of clarity, Absurdity, inattention, and "copping out." Should he feel that these are present with the people he loves, his psychotherapist included, "automatic switching devices" bring exorbitant resistances into play. A patient said to us, "You are bouncing your foot: you do not want to be with me today"; but it was an automatic habit and had no indigenous relevance to her. Any sign of boredom, disinterest, or absence of love stops the growing edge cold, and this is what makes this form of psychotherapy so demanding. Yet such resistances are best handled not necessarily by analyzing them but by reexamining the structure of the relationship at the moment. Confrontations with schizophrenics play a larger part in their treatment than the growth of logical insight—or rather, this is the way to their particular form of insight. And many of them cannot safely be challenged at all at the moment—one waits.

If repressed "secrets" are the phenomenological manifestation of the neurosis, this is much truer for schizophrenia, but in a different way. The schizophrenic believes his is the greatest alchemical secret of all. He codes his language, posture, and behavior so that this secret will never be revealed to anyone. Psychotherapy often becomes a kind of decoding, with the psychotherapist becoming a cryptographer. These secrets rarely turn out to be the "dirty" kind one finds with neurotics. Rather, they have to do with the Absurdity and paradoxy of existence as it is experienced in the very life of the patient. Every conflict of his returns eventually to this fundamental one, and the patient will not allow it to be touched until he assays the customary ones of money, family, love, sex, and so on. All of this is the prelude to getting to the heart of the matter. Rosen errs in that he focuses on tangible conflicts—say, the mother—not always realizing that the philosophy of existence is at stake. The dynamic of the "secret" is aggression, and love and destruction are the antidote, but also the fulminating cap to extinction. The resolution of the unprofitable life style of the schizophrenic involves precisely reaching this nuclear philosophy of existence and altering its direction. Should this be possible, the bizarre thinking, the autism, ambivalence, body delusions, etc., all drop away—they are no longer useful to the patient. Of course, as in the case of Ellen West, suicide is also a possibility as a solution, and Binswanger felt it was an appropriate one for her. Most Americans disagree.

The question of suicide is a particularly important one for schizophrenia. We have said elsewhere that schizophrenics are not distinguished by their special tendency toward suicide, as are the depressives. But schizophrenic patients in long-term therapy are ever-ready for suicide. The configuration of medical ethics is that lives must be saved at any cost. But in the treatment of schizophrenia the patient must symbolically lose his life in order to gain it.[46] And intensive psychotherapy offers them, somewhere along the line, the choice of "doing or dying," and will not allow them to hedge life further by their schizophrenia. The psychotherapist must be prepared to make such a therapeutic offer in good faith and mean it. If he cannot, because of his persona or training, then his patient will probably never be able to reach the ground of his being—to work through his biased existential parameters.

At this point in the treatment, which is the moment of truth, the honesty and humanity of the participants are challenged almost beyond belief. But once surmounted, the patient then goes on to a neurotic status, and the treatment modifies itself to the psychotherapy of the neurosis. At this point we no longer consider the patient schizophrenic.

We have been interested in the fact that physicians who work in state hospitals act as though they know the cure of madness, when actually very little is known of the affective psychoses, schizophrenia, senile psychosis, and their treatment. This pseudo-certainty is reinforced by specially evolved treatment modalities—electric convulsive therapy, highly complex drugs, surgery, water, music, etc.—but for none of these is there an adequate theory of their action. Just try to tell the family of a patient, for example, how ECT works.

In the psychotherapy of schizophrenia it is necessary to depreciate the psychosis as a nosological entity and to counter the established mythology surrounding the psychosis. The patient himself clings to his categorization and is shocked when the psychotherapist ignores his label. Categorization has a way of masking the phenomenon itself and takes over its reality. We have always been concerned that the entire range of psychopathological reactions are forced into a few bins, of which the neuroses, psychoses, and character disorders account for perhaps 90 percent of all the nonorganic diagnoses.

If we were, then, to outline the therapeutic steps necessary to the psychotherapy of schizophrenia as a life style, it would go something like this in outline form and employ actional descriptions where possible.

OUTLINE OF TREATMENT

I. Enlisting the Patient in Treatment
   a. Dissociating from past therapeutic efforts
   b. Admiring and respecting the patient
   c. Dissociating from the operational family
   d. Establishing the image of therapeutic equality
   e. Showing demonic unafraidness
   f. Revealing one's own empathic schizoid or schizophrenic qualities
   g. Extolling life
   h. Intuiting the schizophrenic maneuver
II. Making the Therapeutic Commitment
   a. Demonstrating the need to help
   b. Understanding the patient's coding
   c. Accepting the bizarre and flagrant
   d. Being available and manifesting reliability
   e. Offering freedom and permission-to-be
   f. Becoming expressive and affective
III. Beginning Psychotherapy
   a. Finding an agreed-upon communication and logic
   b. Expressing delusion and hallucination
   c. Intimating "secrets"
   d. Hearing body-image distortions

   e.   Clarifying erogenous zone failure
   f.   Symbolizing nurturance needs
   g.   Becoming hostile
   h.   Furthering transference and identification
IV.   Early Stages
   a.   The rise of countertransference and counteridentification
   b.   Working-through affection and hate
   c.   Beginning confrontation of self-defeating devices
   d.   Insisting and demanding
   e.   Fighting disgust, rejection, and flight
   f.   Preparing for life choices
   g.   Body touching as reinforcement
   h.   Supporting totally as required
   i.   Interpreting first insights; modeling and encountering
V.   The Mid-Stream
   a.   Applying common sense and rationality
   b.   Body communication and its resolution
   c.   Arriving at archetypal insight
   d.   Refusing delusion/hallucination
   e.   Resolving the major therapeutic resistance crisis
   f.   Finding the first social pleasures
   g.   Discovering Eros
   h.   Discovering the meaning of success
   i.   Disowning magic
   j.   Discovery of possible human alternatives
   k.   Offering a deal
   l.   Divorcing self from family (family therapy)
   m.   Wanting to become a therapist
   n.   Synthesizing through sculpture, painting, etc.
   o.   Dream analysis
VI.   Approaching Closure
   a.   Refusing to be psychotic
   b.   Attempting new social ventures
   c.   Attempting love and sexual intercourse
   d.   Finding the meaning of play and humor
   e.   Taking a first vacation

     f. Refusing to code new percepts
     g. Having a regression
     h. Wanting to quit therapy
     i. Manifesting new neurotic symptoms
     j. Deep transference oscillations
     k. Discovering cosmetics, dress, and social display

VII.   Termination
     a. Reduction of visits
     b. Conversing and pastimes
     c. Revaluation of the past schizophrenic life style
     d. Practically handling adaptional problems
     e. Helping with career and profession
     f. Distancing and integrating the nuclear family
     g. Gaining money, status, and social rewards
     h. Seeking group affiliations
     i. Handling neurotic crises as they occur
     j. Verbalizing the new meaning of man
     k. Breaking with the therapist

VIII. The Relapse
     a. Assuring through occasional re-interviews
     b. Approving social progress
     c. Being person-to-person with the patient
     d. Having "small talk"
     e. Having a possible social engagement with the patient
     f. Remaining a friend

No outline of the way we treat schizophrenics can do justice to what actually goes on in the treatment. There is even some doubt about the worth of such an outline. To buttress it qualitatively we make the following observations.

1. What makes this kind of psychotherapy so difficult is the intensity with which all operations take place. There is everything here one finds with neurotics, but more so. It seems necessary for the patient to regularly push all human situations to their outermost limits and in this way distort them or deny them. The watchfulness becomes exorbitant; the participation, over-intense. Sooner or later an uneasiness pervades the treatment, and this is an unnatural feel-

ing for the psychotherapist and he urgently attempts to dispel it. He may even in desperation accuse the patient of making his life unbearable.

It is significant that we never feel fully in love with a schizophrenic patient, as we do with neurotics, until the patient himself changes his schizophrenia to a neurosis. Should such feelings occur in the early stages of psychotherapy, we would question that the patient was schizophrenic. The patient also arouses unconscious impulses in us that have been safely held in check for decades and forces us to confront them. They also force us to question the meaning and value of our socialization. The patient accuses us of the pleasure principle for vanity purposes solely.

2. The psychotherapy of schizophrenia involves working skillfully upon the margins of reality. While we pride ourselves on the hold we have on reality, it is indeed very tenuously held in everyone. Reality, as we know, slips away very rapidly under extreme conditions. The schizophrenic acts as though he wants to shake the psychotherapist's reality, to distort it, and to make it just like his own. And, of course, this would be the certain end of the treatment.

It is most painful to have to constantly monitor one's reality in psychotherapy, to even have to be aware of it, and to have to defend it. If the treatment of schizophrenia by this method is truly egalitarian, who can then say that one reality is superior to another? And, of course, there is no *one* reality. Still, the patient is the patient, and the therapist is not the patient who comes for help. By the nature of things, the reality of the psychotherapist is of the kind that helps the patient, so we must rate it higher at least on this scale of values.

3. We are taught certain linguistic procedures and habits as we grow up, and they then become an indigenous part of the persona or self. These language aspects not only have tremendous social value in getting on in society, but they are the symbolic means by which we receive pleasure and avoid pain. Consider for the moment the schizophrenic's subject-predicate confusion in the statements, "I love you" or "I want to fuck you," if subject and predicate were reversed or distorted. This is of course the Von Domarus principle. It would then be a matter of who gets loved or has sex, and who

does the loving or has sex. This is precisely the schizophrenic's ambivalence, and his language reflects it.

In the psychotherapy of schizophrenia we must at first be prepared to yield not only the subject and predicate order but logical thought itself. The so-called thinking disorder of the schizophrenic is not a disorder at all. It is the patient's way of communication with a world he no longer wants to be a part of; it is his way of highlighting the Absurdity he finds around him. Characteristically he retreats within himself; but if forced to verbalize, why should he be logical, causal, and sequential? We realists ourselves "double-talk," lie, game-play, and change nuances in social relationships as a matter of "getting on" and for polite discourse. But he cannot help coming on straight.

4. So much of the psychotherapy of schizophrenia is so plainly nihilistic, self-defeating, and opportunistic that it often becomes dull or boring. There are long periods when nothing seems to happen. The patient just will not or cannot accept or feel what is so insightfully to be felt, and a stalemate or draw is a regular feature of such work. Who wants to be involved in a perpetual draw? Even in chess this cannot be satisfying. Sooner or later, a stalemate makes every psychotherapist infuriated with his patient and wanting to do him harm. But the personal implications of failing in the treatment and giving in to the demonic are an even worse alternative, so that one plugs on and on. The patient senses this resoluteness and knows he will be ultimately outlasted. Interestingly enough, schizophrenics are good payers and will not disturb psychotherapy because of fees, as do neurotics.

5. Every psychoanalyst and psychotherapist develops his own unique therapeutic style in which he is more or less active or passive. In either case his style is character-consistent and he rarely changes it. As an example, we might contrast the very active rational-emotive approach with the more passive classical Freudian approach. In schizophrenia one's characteristic therapeutic style of passivity or activity is upset, for the patient cannot or will not tolerate such constancy in anyone. And it is upsetting in more ways than this. With them one must at times be active when one feels passive,

and vice versa. This calls for stepping out of character, a conscious effort against the natural self, and for calling upon additional energies not always available or desirable.

6. In addition to the above problem, the psychotherapy of schizophrenia calls for procedural improvisation which at times flies in the face of one's training, custom, ethics, and taboos. Since the patient has more or less left culture behind, the improvisations required will most often be in the direction of asocialization. At first the psychotherapist is reluctant to spontaneously do what his preconscious tells him to do, and he often has some guilt about it. But the need and urgency to solve the problem eventually force him to the unconventional, and its frequent success encourages him. Then he will touch the patient, remove his persona, and do whatever is needed.

7. Psychoanalysis and psychoanalytic psychotherapy, the models for all of the psychotherapies, are historically oriented. It finds the genesis of an intercurrent psychological event in a past real or imagined learning experience. In order to validate or revise that psychological event, it believes that the past must be revaluated or even re-experienced. By some strange juxtaposition of causality, the present moment in the life of the patient becomes slighted (even those moments spent with the psychotherapist), and the future itself not even speculated upon, except perhaps as a formal prognosis. Psychotherapists, by training, are a backward-looking people. The patient's history seemed to work well with neurotics even though the analysis of personal history was often more observed in the breach than in the doing.

But in schizophrenia we have a different state of affairs. In the first place, the schizophrenic's personal history is anathema to him, whereas the neurotic revels in his. In the second place, the schizophrenic has less to recover memorially because he has lived a much less passionate childhood than the neurotic. And finally, the schizophrenic has always been more concerned with his here-now situation, and with his future becoming possibilities, than the neurotic ever could be.

In our psychotherapy of schizophrenia it is impossible, and actually ill advised, to reconstruct the pregenital field of the patient;

and we say this despite full knowledge of the theories of Spitz, Klein, Bowlby, and others. Schizophrenia is not a maternal-child event, but all of those infant, child, and adolescent experiences where social interest arrives on the scene as a major force and the life style is established. The psychotherapist therefore finds that he cannot be as historical as he would like, or has been trained to be, nor can he be historically systematic about it. He must therefore attend more to the here-and-now of the patient's behavior and to the expectations of future status and functioning. These patients in a special way always keep their eye cocked on the future.[47]

CONCLUSION

We wish in conclusion to return to our opening theme, which reiterates the fact that present-day organic, biochemical, and even psychological theories of schizophrenia do not do justice to its phenomena, do not permit us to understand its genesis, and do not provide us with any viable corrective. It is now necessary to return once again to schizophrenia unfettered by binding assumptions and to allow the phenomena to stand forth in their own right. If this can be done, schizophrenia can be seen as a person's highly unique response to a world full of paradoxes and Absurdities he cannot accept or live with. Helping him to relive these on a new basis is the treatment of choice.

REFERENCES

[1] S. Arieti, *Interpretation of Schizophrenia*. New York: Robert Brunner, 1955. See also "Schizophrenia: Other Aspects; Psychotherapy," in *American Handbook of Psychiatry*, S. Arieti (Ed.). New York: Basic Books, Inc., 1959.

[2] H. Spotnitz, *Modern Psychoanalysis of the Schizophrenic Patient*. New York: Grune & Stratton, 1969, p. 1.

[3] C. G. Jung, "Recent Thoughts on Schizophrenia," in *Collected Works*, vol. 3. New York: Pantheon, 1960, p. 255.

[4] S. Arieti, op. cit., pp. 12–15.

[5] R. D. Laing, *The Self and Others*. London: Tavistock, 1961, p. 32.

[6] T. Lidz et al. *Schizophrenia and the Family*. New York: International Universities Press, 1965, p. 430.

[7] B. H. Shulman, *Essays in Schizophrenia*. Baltimore: Williams & Wilkins, 1968, p. 3.

[8] H. Stierlin, *Conflict and Reconciliation*. Garden City, N.Y.: Doubleday, 1969, p. 181.

[9] S. Arieti, op. cit., p. 43.

[10] L. B. Hill, *Psychotherapeutic Intervention in Schizophrenia*. Chicago: University of Chicago Press, 1955, p. 27.

[11] H. Spotnitz, op. cit., p. 28.

[12] H. S. Perry and M. L. Gavel (Eds.). *The Collected Works of Harry Stack Sullivan*. New York: W. W. Norton, 1953, p. 206.

[13] I. A. Caruso, *Existential Psychology*. New York: Herder and Herder, 1964, pp. x–xii.

[14] A. Burton, *Modern Humanistic Psychotherapy*. San Francisco: Jossey-Bass Publishing Co., 1968.

[15] J. Needleman (Ed.), *Being-in-the-World. Selected Papers of Ludwig Binswanger*. New York: Basic Books, Inc., 1963, p. 252.

[16] Ibid., p. 253.

[17] Ibid., p. 225.

[18] Ibid., p. 252.

[19] B. Shulman, op. cit.

[20] R. Cancro, "Schizophrenia: The Unhappy Vicissitudes of a Clinical Concept," in A. R. Kaplan (Ed.), *Genetic Factors in Schizophrenia*. Springfield, Ill.: C. C Thomas, 1971, chapter 24, p. 4.

[21] R. Laing, op. cit., p. 31.

[22] L. Hill, op. cit., p. 23.

[23] Ibid., pp. 66–67.

[24] R. Cancro, op. cit., chapter 24, p. 7.

[25] I. A. Caruso, op. cit., p. xv.

[26] K. A. Adler, "Life Style in Schizophrenia," *J. Indiv. Psychol.*, 1958, *14*, 68–69.

[27] Quoted in H. L. Ansbacher, "Life Style: A Historical and Systematic Review," *J. Individ. Psychol.*, 1967, *23*, 193.

[28] S. M. Miller et al., *Plans and the Structure of Behavior*. New York: Holt, 1960.

[29] A. Camus, *The Rebel*. New York: Vintage Books, 1956, pp. 27–28.

[30] T. Lidz et al., *Schizophrenia and the Family*. New York: International Universities Press, 1965, p. 428.

[31] K. A. Adler, op. cit., p. 72.

[32] C. Kent, *The Puzzled Body*. London: Vision Press, 1969, p. 23.

[33] S. Kierkegaard, *Fear and Trembling and the Sickness unto Death*. New York: Princeton University Press (no date).

[34] J.-P. Sartre, *Being and Nothingness*. London: Methuen, 1957.

[35] L. Binswanger, "The Case of Ellen West," op. cit. (footnote 15), p. 255.

[36] A. Burton, *Interpersonal Psychotherapy*. Englewood Cliffs, N.J.: Prentice-Hall, 1972.

[37] C. Whitaker (Ed.), *Psychotherapy of Chronic Schizophrenic Patients*. Boston: Little, Brown and Co., 1958, p. 167.

[38] A. Burton, op. cit.

[39] C. Whitaker (Ed.), op. cit., p. 163.

[40] See the comments of H. Stierlin in A. Burton and Associates, *Twelve Therapists. How They Live and Find Actualization*. San Francisco: Jossey-Bass Publishing Co., 1972.

[41] J. Needleman (Ed.), op. cit., p. 349.

[42] K. A. Adler, op. cit., p. 72.

[43] A. E. Scheflen, *A Psychotherapy of Schizophrenia: Direct Analysis*. Springfield, Ill.: C. C Thomas, 1961.

[44] A. Ellis, *Growth Through Reason*. Palo Alto: Science and Behavior Books, 1971.

[45] A. Burton (Ed.), *Psychotherapy of the Psychoses*. New York: Basic Books, 1961.

[46] Malone says, "This timing is an important clinical problem. I have found that if you let the patient win before he is ready, you increase at that moment the probability of suicide." Carl Whitaker (Ed.), op. cit., p. 107.

[47] A. Burton, "Hope and Schizophrenia," *Psychoanalytic Review*, 1972, *59*, 609–616.

A PHENOMENOLOGICAL THEORY
OF SCHIZOPHRENIA

Werner M. Mendel

As a student of human behavior and as a clinician, I begin the study of the misfortune and misadventure, the barrenness and the foundering of human existence lived in a schizophrenic life style, by listening. The outcries from such empty and lonely existences begin to convey to the open, compassionate other a sense of the chaos and agony. Listen to these words of various patients[1] and see what you can understand:

> I am like a zombie living behind a glass wall. I can see all that goes on in the world but I can't touch it. I can't reach it. I can't be in contact with it. I am outside. There is nothing there, absolutely nothing.

> Take what you want and let me go.
> I only ask of you, be quick, be quick!
> Do not explore this frozen continent.

I am living a make-believe life and fear I am being asked to pretend even more. It is a real fantasy. It has all the horrors of the fantastic. Should I find myself by giving up myself? Is it instead that myself must change, must become "lovely"?

It is an appearance that I now can only maintain at times and I am being asked not only to adopt it but to replace myself with it. I am different, too. Can't fit into another's pattern. Most people seem to fit into a sort of group pattern but mine is the absolute of such, it seems. I am not this or that, so easily classified as others wish me to be and usually it is their classification they wish me to fit. They call this "caring," "loving" me.

There's something wrong with me. I don't seem to feel about my family like others do. I know this mostly when I talk about my wife and children. I talk about them like my neighbors talk about their cars. I certainly like my family. But if they all went away it wouldn't bother me. They are really quite dispensable. I would just get somebody new, just like my neighbors get new cars.

We forgot that we were not that which we wish to be. We thought without shame and saw the difference only in others and then scorned them. But now it is I who scorns myself and you; and not the others anymore. It wasn't vanity, because that pertains to something one had and we have not. We are not that which we choose, and by forgetting, denying the truth, we cease to exist. Because we are not identical with our visions of ourselves, we deny even our own real existence. You see how I kill myself, murder myself to be other than I am?

To me the world is peopled rather than populated. What I mean by peopled is that it is filled with people much like others' houses are furnished with furniture. It is all the same to me.

I am so scared of doing things and yet want to cram so much in. But I lack the courage to give up; yet, I can't go ahead and change. This whole life seems to be getting ready to die. I am not ready yet, and I am so afraid of what will happen, and you are pushing me to get ready by forgetting like so many people do. Then they die before they use themselves up. The only way I can use myself up is to give myself away. But you and most people don't want what I have to give away. You want me to appear exactly as you pretend to be; to affirm your pretext existence rather than to contribute my own. If only you would give me your real self. I am greedy to enrich my preparation and to accept my real self. Then we would both share in a doubled existence; add another person and it has helped.

> I don't know what makes me tick
> I don't know what makes me sick
> This dying feeling is what I dread
> And I keep wishing I were dead.

I am not yet sure how much control I have over impulses and maybe that is why my husband is so protective. I have caught myself staring, on occasions, and wanting to go on spending sprees, and eating more than I should, but the really frightening symptoms of the past periods when I would have to cling to the wall have not recurred. I am so thankful that, believe me, I haven't forgotten and will never let myself forget to be aware of the danger line.

When I was acting so stiff and wasn't talking it was because I had the feeling that if I moved the whole world might collapse. I knew what you were saying, I knew what was going on in the room around me but I didn't dare budge an inch. I don't know why, but I seemed like I was the center of everything and everything depended on my not moving. It was such a terrible relief when I could begin to lose the feeling that I was so important. I think it wasn't until after you stopped paying so much attention to me that I could stop thinking I was so important. Because when you were paying so much attention to me it made me feel that I was extra important, and it reinforced the feeling I had.

It starts like a feeling of pressure on the back of my neck and head, and then the pressure spreads all over and I feel like I am a bomb that is about to go off. It's like if I looked at myself in the mirror I'd be all puffed up and colored bright red. That's when it is hardest to think clearly. Nobody seems to understand how close I am to blowing up. I feel so damn awful after I have done something or broken something or destroyed something. If only I could keep myself from going that far. There wasn't anybody who seemed to know that I am such a dangerous guy.

What right have you got to tell me that I shouldn't kill myself? Isn't my life mine to do with what I want? If it was any kind of life it would be a different story but I can't ever remember feeling that I was a person whom people ought to be considerate about. I remember my mother used to talk right past me as if I weren't there and even now when I do all the things I am supposed to do for my daughter and my husband, it isn't really like they were reacting to me like a person. I am like a machine that does mother things and wife things. It doesn't seem like they or my mother or anybody ever built anything into me. I guess I just started empty and stayed empty. All the busy work that goes on in living, what people call life, doesn't seem to stick, doesn't seem to last. And besides I don't see why as big a nothing as I am you should consider me worth bothering about, or worth trying to keep me from killing myself. You don't really convince me that you care.

> Nothing is me, nothing is mine.
> I don't live in my body.
> I don't live anywhere.
> My body just is.
> It is just like the strings are pulled
> And it is moved automatically
> But I haven't anything in it.

There is a big hole in my chest. It is so empty it hurts. In fact it is going to explode with emptiness. It is an agony. It simply is that I have to stick something in it. I feel like I have to take a knife or a stick and poke it into my chest to try to fill the emptiness. The big emptiness in me is going to explode.

> Who am I
> I shift with every change in the wind,
> Sometimes cool, sometimes kind,
> Sometimes warm, too often cold.
> Sometimes young, sometimes old.
> Though I dig deep in every you
> Trying to pull out what is true
> For all of us, it is you I see
> I can't find me.

I feel like a thin, empty shell. There is a huge gaping hole in my body. No matter how much I pour into it, it never fills, it never gets any stronger. It is like an eggshell which is empty.

I don't have any feelings. I have nothing except the ache of emptiness.

> She sang softly and sobbed silently.
> So alone, so alone.
> Who cares or wants her?
> Shriveled and torn, so alone.
> Wet, cold, like a smelly corpse.
> So alone! Shouting for help,
> No one can hear
> No one can help.

People are fun but the upkeep is awful—you have to care about them.

> Right and wrong,
> Blame and guilt,
> The flow of love
> Is choked with silt.

It just feels like something is dragging my seeds down and like if I don't hold on to my belly my guts will fall out. Sometimes I realize that this couldn't happen, but the feeling is so strong that it is easy to forget that it wouldn't really happen. Then, if I make myself do the chores you told me to get done, it seems to help me to be more realistic about those physical feelings in my insides. It isn't that the pain goes away—I am still aware of it, but doing something real with my hands seems to make my thoughts more real. But I want you to know that it is an awful and strong feeling. It is pretty hard to keep myself convinced that those terrible things aren't going to happen.

Everything seems so mixed up, so disorganized. I can't seem to fit anything into place or put my fingers on anything. I can't seem to make my thoughts follow one another logically—I just sit in a confused muddle. It is a peculiar drifting feeling but not a pleasant drifting. And then in a way it is almost like a relief when I start to hallucinate. At least I don't just sit confused. I pay attention to what I am hallucinating. Even though it scares hell out of me, I can talk about it now like I knew it was hallucination. When it really happens I don't know, I am not at all sure. It is just like things were unreal in my confusion and then they suddenly become real when the experience happens that I am now later calling hallucination.

I look like a human being but I am really not. I am just a make-believe.

I am making family out of strangers and I am making strangers out of my family.

I look at my arms and they aren't mine. They move without my direction. Somebody else moves them. All my limbs and my thoughts are attached to strings and these strings are pulled by others. I know not who. I have no control. I don't live in me. The outside and I are all the same.

I feel like a smoldering pile of shit.

Even though I am a supposedly healthy young man, no woman wants me. I used the computer last night to look at my problem. After calculating the present population and adult men and women over the age of 18 and below the age of 50, then looking at some sizes of sexual organs in medical books, I have discovered that there are approximately 24,600 kilometers of unused vagina in the United States every night and there isn't even six inches for me anywhere. It is hopeless.

Life is a large ass and quarreling parents, all covered with a large bowel movement.

> Peggy shit sits to spit, stare, and starve.
> She sits solemnly, scorned and so—
> so separated from science.
> Shit stinks smelly. Fat grabs scat.
> Peggy sits alone and shouts.

Alone shoe smell.
She thinks so alone and is so scared.

When I have words the feelings will not come.
But when I truly feel, I am dumb.

I woke up this morning and I knew that it wasn't the world
that was upside down or inside out. It was my eyes. They are
completely turned in the socket. Everything was backward and
inverted. Everything moved that shouldn't move. Everything
that should move, stood still. There was lots of noise and no
sense.

Last night I finally had the chance to put my penis in a lady. It
was all nothing. The whole thing is nothing. It isn't much that's
for sure. I am not going to do it anymore. Never again, there's
nothing there. There is absolutely nothing.

Where I am there is no peace
Anger is my one release
It boomerangs in words that burn
And punish me when they return.

I am a frozen body on a frozen continent. Nothing moves. I stay
away from people because if they push me hard or pull me
hard, my frozen limbs will break off. There is a quiet noise inside of me. I think it is my soul. It still stirs once in awhile. It
isn't frozen all the way, but I know soon I will break.

The curtain going down is caught between
The dingy ceiling and the dusty floor
Although the stage is bare
We sit as if something were there
Still to be seen.
We were the actors and the audience
The authors, too.
Now the play is through
Our recompense
Is nothing, nothing, less than nothing
What did we gain

For twenty years
Bitterness and pain and tears
For what we might have been and we are
Yet we sit afraid to leave
This futile make-believe.

Our cat has kittens
The trees are in leaf
But all I produce
Is more grief.

There is nothing left. Everything is dark and darkness. I cannot live, I can't die, I cannot move. I am completely stuck. My feet are in the quicksand. I do not understand. I do not go under, I do not get up. I cannot get free. I am stuck, stuck, stuck, stuck, stuck, stuck, stuck, stuck, stuck, stuuuucccckkk. . . .

Who feels the black fists of despair
Squeezing the heart
Is my counterpart
Yet the heart beats
Despite defeats,
Sometimes races, sometimes slows
But it goes
This plodding victory is too much to bear.

Only when we have listened to our fellow human beings who cry out in such despair, when we have been with them, lived with them, shared their existences in part, when we have looked into our own soul, and at our response to such agony, such dread, such emptiness, such impairment of self, such blocking of interchange—only then do we begin to understand.

Since earliest history there are descriptions of human existences in pain and agony, filled with emptiness and intermittent implosions.[2] Schizophrenic life lived in chronic dread is portrayed repeatedly in literature as well as in the earliest clinical descriptions. In the sacred literature, schizophrenia is evident in the lives of the saints and the possessed; in legal writings it appears in the code books and in the discussions on responsibility. Observers of human behavior from a sociological, psychological, interpersonal, legal, anatomical, genetic, and biochemical point of view have concerned themselves with schizophrenic existence. Physicians using the familiar medical model described it as a disease and proposed a variety of interventions that were designed to improve function and to prevent the episodic implosions leading to exacerbation of symptoms. But no matter who has described an existence gone awry in this way, nor how they propose to intervene, they always must begin with the same observed phenomena. Schizophrenic existence is lived in constant emptiness with chronic dread. The schizophrenic human being comes away from each contact with himself and with others feeling less competent, less open, and more empty.

Scientists of human living—biologists, psychologists, sociologists, anthropologists—have many approaches to explaining schizophrenia. These explanations always seem to begin with the theoretical bias based on the profession of the explainer. Such explanations tend to include a postulated but unprovable etiology as a starting point. Then an attempt is made to develop a consistent, logical system for pulling together the observations that are inconsistent, illogical, and seemingly impossible to understand. There is, of course, a great difference between explaining a life style and understanding it. Some theoretical approaches, because of the logical sequences of theory building, make good explanations. Yet these explanations do not help us to understand.

However I choose to explain schizophrenia, I cannot understand it, I cannot comprehend schizophrenic life style in human existence, unless I go back to the phenomena of behavior which I can observe. The verbal and nonverbal behavior, the reporting from the individual who lives schizophrenia, my feelings and thoughts and those of the others who come in contact with schizophrenic existence—all have to become part of any possible basic understanding. We must begin our attempt at understanding by throwing away our books and our theories and going back to the human being who lives a schizophrenic existence.

Clinical descriptions, such as thought-process disorder, impaired reality testing, shallow interpersonal relationships, or defective ego functioning, do not portray the despair and the agonies of those who exist in schizophrenic lives.

MODELS FOR INTERVENTION

Only when we have seen the distress can we begin to understand and perhaps have some first idea of how to help. The conduct of the helping transaction depends on such understanding. How to relate to such existences and how to deal with our own pain vis-à-vis such agony can be understood only in the intimacy of a loving, caring human encounter.

The intervention which the human being who lives a schizophrenic existence engenders in others frequently has little to do with what is going on in him or with his needs. The response seems geared to the needs of others, *their* professions, *their* life style, and to those things which they habitually do rather than what needs to be done. There are five models of intervention based on the preoccupation and profession of the intervener rather than on the need of human beings living schizophrenic life styles.

The first of these is the *legal model.* In this model the acts, the feelings, the thoughts, and the communication of human beings are seen as having to comply with a codable norm. When they do not conform, the individual who does not comply is called a criminal. The intervention in his life is called a system of jurisprudence. The people who intervene are called policemen, judges, lawyers, and prison wardens. The transaction is one of crime and determination of guilt. Restitution is made in terms of punishment, parole, and expunging.

The second model is the *medical model.* Problems of human existence are defined as illness. The transaction is one of cure. The person who lives a schizophrenic existence in dread and fear and emptiness is called a patient. Those who intervene are called doctors, nurses, psychiatrists, therapists, psychologists, and ancillary (female slave) personnel. Drugs are used to alter tissue function. Physical methods of intervention are used to alter anatomical and physiological states. The places where the helping transactions are carried out are hospitals, clinics, facilities, and offices. If and when the life style changes, the "patient" is called cured, recovered, reconstituted, or remitted.

The third model is the *educational model,* in which the problem of schizophrenic life style is explained as having resulted from childhood experiences that have been left out or gone awry. The process of repair is reeducation or a corrective emotional experience[3] or conditioning, or retraining or resocialization. The schizophrenic life style is viewed as an educational defect resulting from such educational mishaps as double-binds, traumas, and personality. The person who lives a schizophrenic life style is a student or client. The one who intervenes is a teacher or educator, or a retraining manager, or a milieu director, or a psychologist, or the director of a corrective emotional experience. The transaction is one of unlearning, learning, and relearning. The outcome of the transaction is the result of having had experiences which change attitudes, feelings, thoughts, and behavior due to new learning.

The fourth approach is the *rehabilitation model.* In this model, much like in the medical model, the human being living a schizophrenic existence is seen as having a defect. The defect may be due to heredity, injury, sickness, or whatever. There is no attempt made at repairing the defect but, rather, taking what is left of function and rehabilitating those functions so they can take over some of the functions that are missing and assumed to be missing forever. The person who is helped is called the client or patient. Those who rehabilitate the clients are rehabilitation therapists, vocational counselors, physical therapists, social workers, social therapists, and social space engineers and psychiatrists. The technique consists in teaching clients how to think, how to feel, how to act, how to be something which they are not—in other words, to act "as if"[4] they did not have a schizophrenic life style. Success is measured in terms of the ability of the client to hide his schizophrenic life style and to comply and conform to the majority culture in which he lives.

In the *social repair model* the issues of a schizophrenic existence are seen as a social problem in society. The people who intervene are called sociologists, social workers, politicians, and members of various volunteer service organizations. They view the difficulty of schizophrenic existence as being a difficulty in society which must be altered by social manipulation of the psychosocial space surrounding the schizophrenic existence. The approach is one of social action and environmental manipulation. The end result of this intervention is deemed successful if the immediate psychosocial space has been adjusted to the human being who lives a schizophrenic life style, and if both have become more congruent in their juxtaposition.

In all five of these approaches the view of schizophrenic existence, the theories and explanations of the difficulty, and the type of interventions are entirely dependent on the model of thinking of the one who makes the decisions. The interventions are based on his professional affiliation, which reflects his life style and training, rather than on an understanding of the schizophrenic life style or the needs of the schizophrenic existence. The techniques of intervention, which include education, repair, forced relationships, changing of social systems, administration of agents to change physiology and anatomy, and personal incarceration, may or may not be helpful. Proponents of each of these five models develop a theory of etiology and focus on a different aspect of being human.

How we view being human will also determine how we choose to view the living of a schizophrenic existence. One such view of humanness which has become very popular in recent years tends to focus on being human and living a schizophrenic existence from the average point of *the behavior* of the individual human being who lives a schizophrenic existence. The human being is seen as an incomprehensible black box into which there is certain stimulus input and out of which comes behavior, both verbal and nonverbal. The behavior is seen as the problem; changing the behavior is seen as the issue. The result is judged in terms of the changed behavior.

A second view focuses on the inside of the black box. There are certain *psychological functions,* including techniques of management of anxiety, ways of thinking, ways of feeling, ways of perceiving, which intervene between the stimulus input and the behavior output. These functions and techniques are not observable and are inferred only. Those who choose to focus on this theory attempt to change these postulated psychological functions of schizophrenic existence.

A third view, one that results from a focus on the *biological substructure* of being human, is that the black box consists of anatomy, biochemistry, and physiology. All of being human and being schizophrenic can be explained in what happens in the black box in terms of replicable anatomical, biochemical, and physiological events. Those who look at schizophrenic life style with this biological approach attempt to intervene by changing physiology and anatomy, hoping that this will alter the sequence of input and output out of the black box.

A fourth theoretical bias is the *experiential* one. Its adherents believe that the black box has been formed out of an *aggregate of experiences* and that it can be altered by another aggregate of experiences. To these theoreticians the black box is simply a history which has accumulated and which can be altered by a new history.

A fifth approach is the *interpersonal approach.* Proponents of this view see the difficulty of schizophrenic existence only as a manifestation of interpersonal difficulties. They see the black box constantly redefined by its position in relation to other black boxes. The issue of intervening thus becomes one of providing a new, different, and more useful juxtaposition for the schizophrenic black box to other black boxes.

In all these models and explanations, it is easy to forget the totality of being human. We must always come back to the human being who lives schizophrenia, and begin our understanding with an empathic willingness to relate and observe. All of these models, these interventions, these techniques, are based on what the interveners need and want and believe. They usually have little to do with the schizophrenic existence.

THE DISEASE MODEL

Now let us look in some detail at the best of the medical models of schizophrenia, which view this painful and ineffective human condition as an illness.

At the turn of the twentieth century, all disease models followed the postulates of Robert Koch. A physician could feel assured that he knew the cause of the disease when he had fulfilled the four Koch postulates. The prototype for all disease was that of bacteriological disease. First the disease had to be described and identified; then the pathogenic organism had to be isolated; next a healthy host organism was inoculated with the pathogenic agent; and then the disease was reproduced in the host animal. When the disease was reproduced in the host, the pathogenic agent was again isolated. When these Koch's postulates had been fulfilled, the physician felt satisfied that he knew the cause of the illness. To some extent the early ideas of Freud's psychopathology come from this era. Those who today believe in the exclusive organic etiology of schizophrenia hold to this view and would insist on fulfilling Koch's postulates. They believe that a schizococcus, or its equivalent, causes schizophrenia. In the early years of his work in psychopathology, Freud believed (under the influence of Charcot) that a specific traumatic event caused the disease. He believed that if the trauma could be removed (abreaction), the disease could be cured and the same trauma would cause similar disease in other hosts.

Today we are more knowledgeable about the disease process and know that even the simplest of bacteriological diseases, such as pneumococcus pneumonia or tuberculosis, are not caused simply by a bacillus. They are caused by many factors, *including* the bacillus.

The next model of disease which became prominent in medicine was the adaptational model. This theory of disease is best exemplified by the work of Hans Selye,[5] who saw diseases as failed attempts at adaptation. The response to the injurious process becomes the disease itself. Physiologically, the body responds to physical insult or injury in certain limited ways, including the rubor, calor, dolor, and tumor (redness, fever, pain, and swelling). Selye described more complex adaptational responses to stress and was able to show how the disease is in fact the hypertrophied, maladaptive normal response to the injury or infection. This model is essentially the model utilized in later Freudian theory, in which defenses against anxiety become disease. Either as the result of excessive stress over long periods, resulting in chronically hyperactive defenses, or as the result of the disorganization of defensive systems, the defenses result in maladaptation rather than adaptation. In these terms, schizophrenia is seen as a maladaptive, defensive response to life, resulting in a diseased life style.

The most useful version of the modern disease model is the one developed by S. Wolf and H. Wolff.[6] They maintain that medicine has asked the wrong questions. It makes no sense to ask "What causes this illness?" because in fact there is no simple cause of illness. Tuberculosis is not caused by a tubercle bacillus, but by a complex set of factors that include the tubercle bacillus. Tuberculosis is caused by genetic predisposition, social factors, nutritional state, emotional condition, environment, *and* the tubercle bacillus. This theory has been called the theory of the relevant etiological factor. Wolf and Wolff suggest that instead of "What causes this illness?" we must ask, "What conditions taken *together* in *this* patient at *this time* make it possible for these symptoms to emerge? What genetic factors, what biological, physiological, economic, work, social, psychological factors and what educational-family conditions all come together at this time (not at some other time) in this patient (not in some other patient) to give us the picture we see here before us now?" Or, to translate it from the physical disease model to the psychiatric disease model, we might say, "What conditions taken together in this patient at this time make it possible for this behavior pattern, these feelings, these attitudes, to emerge?" This, then, lets us sidestep the important—though unsolved—question of etiology in schizophrenia and allows us immediately to go to the important issue of intervention. When we have identified all that we know in each of these areas about each patient (the genetic, biochemical, social, educational, psychological, and familial areas), we intervene in each area to alter conditions so as to be helpful to the patient-client. Then we might well say about a specific patient that we must identify his biochemical problems, his social problems, his economic problems. We must identify and study in detail his psychological mechanisms, his familial-psychosocial space, and his genetic predisposition. After we have identified these, we must see in each area what alterations we can make. As we make alterations in each of these facets, the total person will change so that we can help to alter behavior attitudes, feelings, and life style and can claim a successful treatment response in the medical model.

However, in order to successfully outline a treatment program in the medical model, we must first agree that we are dealing with a disease consisting of signs and symptoms that are clearly definable. At first it seems easy to suggest that schizophrenia is indeed a disease. It is particularly easy for those of us who understand the human condition from the perspective of the profession of medicine. But when we are with and listen to and relate to schizophrenic life styles, the disease model no longer suffices. It is absolutely essential that we thoroughly understand what we can about the life style of the schizophrenic existence: the difficulties, the strengths, the weaknesses. Most of us who come to the problem of understanding human distress from the medical model tend to focus on psychopathology; that is, we tend to focus on those things which are wrong with a human being. This is a curious way of approaching a helpful intervention because, in fact, we will not work with the person's defects or difficulties but will work with those of his aspects which are intact, which are right about him, which are his ego strengths, which are the least regressed aspect of his life style. Contrary to the usual type of diagnostic criteria in the medical model, it is essential for us to understand what the strengths of the schizophrenic existence are—how these can be utilized to help in alleviating distress, in filling emptiness, in relieving panic, and in repairing loneliness. We also must understand that although there are many common characteristics in schizophrenic existences, there are also significant individual differences. After reminding ourselves of these individual differences, we can then go on with attempting to observe, describe, and understand patterns of similarity and patterns of difference between schizophrenic existences and nonschizophrenic existences.

Observations about schizophrenic existences were developed by Eugen Bleuler,[7] who popularized the term "schizophrenia." It was his view that schizophrenia was essentially an organic disease of the central nervous system, based either on chemical or anatomical defects, and that schizophrenia always included four categories of signs and symptoms. These are his well-known "Four A's." The first is the the difficulty in thinking characterized by loosening of *associations,* which is manifested by tangentiality and non sequitur thought processes. To Bleuler this defect in the mechanism of thinking was basic. The second "A" is *ambivalence.* He noted that people living a schizophrenic existence seemed to have major and immobilizing ambivalence. Even though ambivalence (having two opposing feelings or desires at the same time) is part of the human condition, in schizophrenic patients the ambivalence is so immobilizing that in fact the patient gets stuck in the middle, like the Cartesian donkey between the two haystacks. All is equivalent; the patient cannot move either forward or backward or sideways, according to Bleuler. His third "A," *autism,* is the patient's primary preoccupation with his inner space—with his subjective reality. The patient generally has disengaged himself from the external world of consensually validated reality. The fourth "A" applies to the *altered affect* of the patient, which Bleuler described as both flat and inappropriate. By flat, he meant that the patient does not show what seems to be usual mood modulation; by inappropriate he meant that frequently the patient displays a mood which does not seem to be tied to the content of his thinking. Bleuler thought these "Four A's" were the primary symptoms—that all other symptoms or signs seen in schizophrenic existences were secondary. To Bleuler, delusions are based on thought process disorder (loosening of associations), hallucinations are based on the rejection of consensually validated reality, and the idiosyncratic approach to life is based on the patient's autism. Even though the "Four A's" are much more useful as an approach to describing schizophrenia than simply the concept of one agent causing a disease, such as a schizococcus or a specific biochemical presence or absence of compound, they in fact take into account only a very narrow range of the psychosocial space of the patient. Every experienced clinician who has lived with a schizophrenic existence knows that in fact the affect is not flat at all. It is most usually mercurial, wildly fluctuating, with the formation of chaotic and intense relationships that move from positive to negative and back to positive in a matter of minutes. Furthermore, the experienced clinician knows that difficulty in thinking is not specific to schizophrenia but occurs in all human beings under stress. The loose associations may be a manifestation of an altered ability by an individual to handle "normal" stress. The ambivalence thought to be fundamental by Bleuler might easily be judged not to be any greater in the schizophrenic existence than in that of any other human being—perhaps the difference is in what the schizophrenic patient does about his ambivalence, how he responds to it, and how he deals with it. The autism is highly variable, fluctuating both in normal and in schizophrenic existences. After all, no one would accuse Martin Buber[8] of being schizophrenic; yet one of his important statements is that the only reality is the subjective reality of personal experience. With this statement he sides with the idiosyncratic interpretation of consensually validated reality.

In order to understand schizophrenic existence in all its multifaceted complexity, we cannot use a simple biological approach nor can we simply use the wide symptom classification approach of Bleuler. We must do what Sydenham[9] said so long ago to his students of medicine: "Throw away your books and theories and return to the patient's bedside." We must try to understand in infinite detail those phenomena which we have chosen to group together descriptively under the heading of *schizophrenic existence* and *schizophrenic life style.*

We can summarize the observed phenomena in the best tradition of French phenomenology.[10] We can then attempt to understand the difficulties and agonies of schizophrenic existence and design a strategy of rescue and help based on these phenomena.

The three primary categories in which we can summarize all of our observations and descriptions of phenomena of schizophrenic life style are: (1) failure of historicity; (2) chaotic, expensive, and ineffective management of anxiety; and (3) painful interpersonal misadventures.

HISTORICITY

In the course of a nonschizophrenic existence, the human being differentiates himself from his surroundings through a series of sequential relationships with others. Some remnant of each of these relationships remains part of his existence, and all future relationships are built upon it. The event of prior relationships becomes incorporated into his existence as part of his history, his experience, and his anticipation. In a way, part of each experience sticks to the individual's ribs, like a good meal. He has eaten the relationship and some of it stays with him. How much of it stays with him, how important that relationship is, depends in part on how early it occurs, what other similar relationships are available to draw upon, how highly valued the relationship was, how much pain or pleasure it gave, and so forth.

In the schizophrenic existence there seems to be no remaining lived history at any one moment. When the experience stops, it is as though none of it stuck to the ribs of the schizophrenic existence. This is the case even if the experience has lasted over a long period. One can see this very clearly in the relationship of others to schizophrenic existences. A nonschizophrenic existence has a relationship with a schizophrenic existence over a decade or more, and it seems meaningful to both. Then it terminates for some reason. Within hours, the schizophrenic existence has nothing left of the relationship, whereas the nonschizophrenic existence has memories, pains, separation anxiety, loss, and remembered pleasure and sadness. It is as though none of the previous ten years of intimacy and authentic meaningful interaction stuck to the ribs of the schizophrenic existence. It is all gone. It is as though the plug has been pulled out of the bathtub and once again it is empty. When the water has stopped running and it becomes empty, the tub has run out.

It is clear that the consequences of such failure of historicity are most serious and create the major problem of intervening in a helpful way. This is particularly true because we use a human relationship as the bridge to the schizophrenic existence in alleviating the pain and agony of schizophrenic life style. It is as though the schizophrenic existence has no memory. Each experience has to start anew. Each relationship is the first and only one. It is this failure of historicity which contributes to the observation that the human being living a schizophrenic life is constantly exhausted simply from managing the everyday affairs of living. This exhaustion becomes understandable when we remember that each day he arises for the first time, he washes for the first time, he discovers breakfast for the first time, he manages his life's day for the first time. He is unable to draw on any prior experience, unable to have any faith in himself or in the world. It is this failure of historicity which is fundamental to the totally impaired self-esteem so frequently seen in schizophrenic life. Erwin Straus[11] has described the peculiar stiff motion and walking of a person with schizophrenia. Such peculiar walking is one of the consequences of the failure of historicity and the related inability to have faith in the world. All who have lived with schizophrenic life know of the peculiar angularity of schizophrenic motion, the peculiar way of sitting or moving through space, the strange gait, the lack of the associated arm movements in walking. This physical clumsiness and awkwardness (not secondary to phenothiazine) become understandable when we recognize that walking is motion on faith. Each step we take is made with the assumption that the ground is there waiting for our foot. At the beginning, we look, we stumble, but we learn. Soon we walk automatically, looking ahead but not looking ahead with each step. The schizophrenic existence cannot take this step of faith. This results in the clumsy, awkward gait. Each step for the schizophrenic existence is a brand new ordeal to discover again and again whether the ground is there waiting.

Another way to describe the difficulty caused by lack of available historicity and lived experience by the schizophrenic existence is to compare schizophrenic life style to nonschizophrenic life style. There are no guarantees in life; indeed, it is possible that tomorrow morning the sun will not rise. Most of us, however, accept on faith, at least at an operational level, that tomorrow will come and the sun will rise for the world even if not for us. We plan our lives in accordance with this faith. We think, we plan, we save, we buy insurance, we make commitments, and we anticipate. The schizophrenic existence has difficulty with all such anticipation and planning. He does not know whether the sun will rise tomorrow even though he does know it has done so for billions of years. He gets "hung up" on the possibility that there is no guarantee that the sun will rise tomorrow, and he has to live his life at this moment without being able to take the small leap of faith into the future by believing that tomorrow will come.

This problem of historicity, which also results in a total closure of the future, makes the experience of time different for the schizophrenic existence than for the nonschizophrenic existence. In the nonschizophrenic existence the experience of time can be viewed as circular, in which the present moment is experienced in action and moves on to remembered and incorporated past. Time is experienced as a moving circle, each moment moving from the future through the present into the past. This orderly flow of experience is the reality of historicity. The schizophrenic existence is empty, having no past, having no future, having only the present. Studies on the experience of time in schizophrenic life demonstrate how the passage of time —living of time, and the experience of time—is basically altered in these life styles.[12] Since experience and relationships are built on time sequence experienced together and lived together, it is clear that here again is one of the major difficulties and obstacles in finding a way of intervening helpfully and alleviating the distress or pain of schizophrenic existence. The schizophrenic existence has no past. It has no history. It has no future. It has no anticipation, no faith, and no self-reliance. All of these lacks are secondary to the failure of historicity. The signs and symptoms of low self-esteem, of panic, of impaired interpersonal relationships, of failure of object-relationships, of impaired self-boundaries (ego), of failure to differentiate between what has occurred and what was thought, fantasied, dreamed, and hallucinated; the inability to be goal-directed in behavior, to plan; the failure to learn from experience, to benefit from the corrective emotional experience—all of these are secondary to the primary failure of historicity.

FAILURE OF ANXIETY MANAGEMENT

The difficulty in managing anxiety is seen in every schizophrenic existence. It seems to be superimposed on all aspects of living life. It is related and to some extent perhaps dependent on the failure of historicity since it appears that schizophrenic existence never really learns how to manage anxiety economically. The schizophrenic existence expends a huge amount of energy in attempting to deal with anxiety and always it fails. The result of this failure is a constant need to work at coping and failing. Therefore, these human beings are tired and worn out all the time. They have a multitude of symptoms—a panneurosis. Significant others who live with schizophrenic existences note how difficult it is for them just to conduct the ordinary everyday business of living. It is exhausting. Their bodies are wracked with pain just from getting through the day. They do not have the energy to maintain even the borders of inside and outside.

The nonschizophrenic existence usually learns to manage anxiety in early childhood by identifying with significant others and thus adopting their techniques. Other anxiety management techniques are culturally determined by social class membership, and are subject to fashion and the times. All of this implies the need for a certain capacity for historicity which the schizophrenic existence lacks. Thus, in this area too, one of the major problems is the apparent (not real) lack of memory, lack of historicity, lack of ability to prepare by anticipation. Because of the failure of the past to influence the present, the absence of future, and the enslavement by the present, the schizophrenic existence is severely handicapped in its management of anxiety. Beyond this problem with historicity in regard to the management of anxiety, there is further difficulty. The schizophrenic existence does not seem to have the motivation, the wherewithal, or the techniques to learn to manage anxiety economically. Anxiety seems just as painful and stressing to the schizophrenic existence as to the nonschizophrenic existence, but the amount of energy necessary to manage anxiety is much greater in a schizophrenic life style and the effectiveness of the technique is much less than in the nonschizophrenic life style. It is as though the nonschizophrenic existence can manage many more ergs of anxiety with one-tenth erg of anxiety-managing devices (defenses). The schizophrenic existence manages one erg of anxiety with 100 ergs of anxiety-managing devices, and then the devices do not work in binding anxiety. The anxiety still remains, not very much reduced, and the existence is exhausted. This phenomenon has been described clinically in such terms as panneurosis, neurasthenia, withdrawal, and stupor. It seems as though the techniques of managing anxiety, which work for everyone else, do not work for the schizophrenic existence even after exhausting and depleting attempts. The management of anxiety is so impaired and so expensive that the description of schizophrenic existence always seems to include such terms as tenuous, fragile, unstable. Nonschizophrenic existence can walk the path of life with relative ease and comfort and rest occasionally. A nonschizophrenic existence might stumble on a boulder which appears in its life path. Usually, the existence manages to climb over the boulder and to go on. Schizophrenic existence, however, stumbles and falls over pebbles. Often the pebbles are so small that the nonschizophrenic existence doesn't even see them. But to the schizophrenic existence these pebbles—the ordinary, everyday situations—can lead to an exhausting disintegration of the person in proportions which no one could imagine who has not seen it occur. Just getting through a day of life is an almost impossible task.

INTERPERSONAL MISADVENTURE

This category of phenomena observed in schizophrenic existence to some extent follows from the previous two. It is clear that if the person has no history and does not have available to him the ability to anticipate the future, he must enter into each relationship with another human being, reinventing himself each day and each moment.

Furthermore, schizophrenic existence, because it has no historicity, enters the relationship with the tremendous disadvantage of low self-esteem.[13] Esteem is built from successfully having managed life. If there is no history available to managing life, not to say anything about successfully managing life, then each interpersonal relationship is entered into each moment for the first time. There is nothing to lean on, nothing to compare to, no learned skills to bring to the transaction. When we add to this the difficulties brought into the interpersonal space as the result of the second category—namely, the expensive and ineffective approach to managing anxiety—

we can see how the interpersonal transaction is doomed from the beginning. The human being in a schizophrenic existence has impaired self-esteem because he has no living history, because he cannot experience the anticipatory affect of the future, because he cannot take advantage of friendship offered. The best he can hope for is the solitary, cold comfort of the formalized juxtaposition of two existences rather than the intimacy of a relationship. The painful, expensive management of anxiety in the schizophrenic existence interferes in all ways with the establishment, maintenance, or alteration of the schizophrenic existence's relationship with other existences. But beyond the effect of the lack of historicity and the exhaustion of managing anxiety expensively and ineffectively, the interpersonal transactions of schizophrenic existences are severely impaired. The schizophrenic existence comes away from each human encounter feeling a little worse about himself, a little worse about the other, and a little more hopeless about the world. This hopelessness, which results from the inability to experience the future in its anticipatory influence on the present, is a serious impairment in the interpersonal transaction. Thus, having come away from each interpersonal transaction feeling worse about himself and the world, having lost faith, and having lost prior experience, the schizophrenic existence can take no risks in the psychosocial interpersonal space with anyone else.

The consequences of the painfulness of interpersonal transactions for the schizophrenic existence are most serious both for the existence and for the attempted intervention by others. Since the schizophrenic existence comes away from each relationship feeling a little worse about everything, there is no reason for an attempt to reach out for help even when others offer it. Yet the major vehicle for intervening is that of a human relationship. The schizophrenic existence has been likened to the person who lives in a glass prison, pounding on the walls, unable to be heard, yet very visible. Even when things go well in schizophrenic existence, it is the interpersonal area which remains awry.

The subjective and objective phenomena comprising the world of schizophrenia can be grouped in these three major categories which we have described: (1) *historicity;* (2) *the management of anxiety;*

and (3) *interpersonal psychosocial space*. The schizophrenic existence fails in each of these. In historicity it suffers the pain and agony of having to start each experience *de novo*. No experiences stick
to him, no experiences become part of his history. It is as though he
had a specific memory deficit for personal history. The memory
deficit closes the past to him and closes the future to him, and
makes him a victim of his present moment of action each second of
his life.

His approach to anxiety management is so chaotic and so expensive and so totally ineffective that he is tired and exhausted from
the ordinary tasks of everyday life. Even though he expends fantastic amounts of psychic energy, he has nothing to show for it except
his tiredness. His anxieties are not bound, his dread is not dimin-
ished, his panic constantly haunts him and whips him to the point
of disorganization, nonfunction, and intrapersonal chaos. It is as
though he were on a rack constantly stretched by his anxiety. He is
always stretched beyond his limit, hoping for death yet dreading it,
wishing for nonexistence yet unable to tolerate it, ready to give all
for a moment of peace. Yet he goes on suffering, exhausted and ineffective.

His interpersonal relationships add much to his anxiety because
they are impaired by his lack of historicity and the chaos of his life
and his existence. Each one is more painful than the last. Even
though each interpersonal relationship has finished, the pain seems
to linger on and the pool of pain, not remembered but felt, constantly drowns him in the depths of despair.

Phenomenologically, the lack of historicity, the expensive and ineffective anxiety management, and the constantly painful interpersonal relationships are the primary difficulties of the schizophrenic
existence. A further look at these, particularly in the eloquent words
of a schizophrenic existence, makes it clear that the three primary
categories of difficulty of the schizophrenic existence can be better
understood when we realize that of these three, the most basic defect is the failure of historicity. The other two primary difficulties
(painful interpersonal relationships and ineffective anxiety management) are partially the result of this basic failure of historicity.

This phenomenological theory can be best understood when we

go back to observing the patient. Below are the words of Ellen West, a schizophrenic girl described in great detail by Ludwig Binswanger in his paper "The Case of Ellen West"[14] (translated from German by the author).

Ellen West, a highly literate patient, lived a schizophrenic existence until she committed suicide at the age of thirty-three. She expresses her difficulties with historicity in eloquent words. Her difficulty manifests itself in the feeling of emptiness that cannot be filled. There is nothing there. To fill this emptiness the schizophrenic existence lives as if it were possible to fill. She stuffs her existence with activity and with work. She stuffs her body with food. She has difficulty in differentiating between inside and outside, between me and they, between thoughts, fantasies, delusions, hallucinations, dreams, and wishes on the one side, and action and events on the other. It shows itself in the difficulty she has with her body image and in the diffusion of the borders into the outside world. The failure of historicity manifests itself in the need to establish the personal borders and to maintain the borders, while simultaneously being unable to maintain the borders. The future is closed, the past unavailable; all is hopelessness and emptiness. When she was eighteen she wrote in her diary:

> What would we be without work, what would become of us? I think they would soon have to enlarge the cemeteries for those who went to death of their own accord. Work is the opiate for suffering and grief.
>
> When all the joints in the world threatened to fall apart, when the light of our happiness is extinguished and our pleasure in life lies wilting, only one thing saves us from madness: work. Then we throw ourselves into a sea of duties as into lethe, and the roar of its waves is to drown out the death-knell pealing in our heart.
>
> When the day is done with its haste and unrest, and we sit by the window in the growing twilight, the book will fall from our hand, we stare into the distance, into the setting sun, and old pictures rise up before us. The old plans and hopes, none of which have been realized, the boundless barrenness of the world and our infinite minuteness stands before our tired soul.

Then the old question crowds to our lips, "What for?—why all this? Why do we strive and live, forgotten after a short span of time, only to moulder in the cold earth?"

At such a time spring up quickly, and well for you if there is a call for you, and work with both hands, until the shapes of the night disappear. Oh, work, you are indeed the blessing of my life!

She goes on to say that she would like to gain fame—great, undying fame. After hundreds of years her name should still ring out on the lips of mankind. Then she would not have lived in vain. She cries to herself:

Oh, smother the murmuring voices with work! Fill up your life with duties. I will not think so much—my last address shall not be the madhouse! And when you have worked and toiled, what have you accomplished? What prevails around us and below us is still so much of boundless distress! There they are dancing in a brightly lighted hall, and outside the door a poor woman is starving to death. Starving! Not a crust of bread comes to her from the table of plenty. Did you observe how the fine gentleman, while speaking, slowly crushed the dainty bread in his hand? And outside in the cold a woman cried out for a dry crust! And what's the use of brooding on it? Don't I do the same? . . .

She tries to fill her emptiness. She tries to find answers:

I am filled with a consuming thirst to learn and I have already had a glimpse of the "secret of the universe."

At age twenty-one she is married and has two children. But she cannot grasp it. It does not stick to her ribs. Her border problems, her emptiness, are described in the following. Her paralyzing dread and despair continue. In her diary she writes:

I have not kept a diary for a long time; but today I must again take my notebook in hand; for in me there is such a turmoil and ferment that I must open a safety valve to avoid bursting out in wild excessives. It is really sad that I must translate all this force and urge to action into unheard words instead of powerful deeds. It is a pity of my young life, a sin to waste my sound mind. For what purpose did nature give me health and ambition? Surely not to stifle it and hold it down and let it languish in the chains of humdrum living, but to serve wretched humanity. The iron chains of commonplace life: the chains of conventionality, the chains of property and comfort, the chains of gratitude and consideration, and, strongest of all, the chains of love. Yes, it is they that hold me down, hold me back from a tempestuous revival, from the complete absorption into the world of struggle and sacrifice for which my whole soul is longing. Oh God, dread is driving me mad! Dread which is almost certainty! The consciousness that ultimately I shall lose everything: all courage, all rebelliousness, all drive for doing.

Yet in a poem she writes:

> The only longing left to my eyes is that for the darkness.
> Where the glaring sun of life does not shine.

Other diary entries read:

> If thou still rulest behind clouds, Father, then I beseech thee, take me back to thee!
> All courage, all rebelliousness, all drive for doing; that itch— my little world—will make me flabby, and fainthearted, and beggardly as they are, themselves.
> Live? No, vegetate! Do you actually preach making concessions? I will make no concessions! You realize that the existing social order is rotten, rotten down to the root, dirty and mean; but you do nothing to overthrow it. But we have no right to close our ears to the cry of misery and to walk with closed eyes past the victims of our system! I am twenty-one years old and am supposed to be silent and grin like a puppet. I am no puppet. I am a human being with red blood and a woman with quivering heart. And I cannot breathe in this atmosphere of hypocrisy and cowardice, and I mean to do something great and must get a little closer to my ideal, my proud ideal. Will it cost tears? Oh, what shall I do, how shall I manage it? It boils and pounds

in me, it wants to burst the outer shell! Freedom! Revolution!

No, no, I'm not talking claptrap, I'm not thinking of the liberation of the soul; I mean the real, tangible liberation of the people from the chains of their oppressors. Shall I express it still
more clearly? I want a revolution, a great uprising to spread
over the entire world and overthrow the whole social order. I
should like to forsake home and parents like a Russian nihilist,
to live among the poorest of the poor, and make propaganda for
the great cause. Not for the love of adventure! No, no! Call it
unsatisfied urge to action if you like, indomitable ambition.
What has the name to do with it? To me, it is as if this boiling
in my blood was something better. Oh, I am choking in this pet-
ty commonplace life. Bloated self-satisfaction or egotistical greed,
joyless submissiveness or crude indifference; these are the plants
which thrive in the sunshine of the commonplace. They grow and
proliferate, and like weeds they smother the flower of longing
which germinates among them.

Everything in me trembles with dread, dread of the adders
of my every day, which would coil about me with their cold
bodies and press the will to fight out of me. But my exuberant
force offers resistance. I shake them off, I *must* shake them off.
The morning must come after the siege of nightmares.

She continues to talk about her difficulty with others and her
self-image:

My inner self is so closely connected with my body that the
two form a unity and together constitute my "I." My unlogical,
nervous, individual "I."

She feels herself to be absolutely worthless and useless and is in
dread of everything: the dark and the sun, stillness and noise. She
expresses the difficulty with her self-esteem and feels herself on the
lowest rung of the ladder which leads to the light, degraded to a
cowardly, wretched creature:

I despise myself.

In a poem she writes during this period, grim distress sits at her grave, ashy pale—sits and stares, does not flinch or budge; the birds grow mute and flee, the flowers wilt before its ice-cold breath.

She further expresses her difficulty with self-esteem in a poem entitled "Evil Thoughts":

> One time we were your thinking,
> Your hoping pure and proud!
> Where now are all your projects,
> The dreams that used to crowd?
>
> Now all of them lie buried,
> Scattered in wind and storm,
> And you've become a nothing,
> A timid earthy worm.
>
> So then we have to leave you,
> To dark night we must flee;
> The curse which fell upon you
> Has made us black to see.
>
> If you seek peace and quiet,
> Then we'll come creeping nigh
> And we'll take vengeance on you
> With our derisive cry.
>
> If you seek joy and gladness,
> We'll hurry to your side;
> Accusing you and jeering
> We'll e'er with you abide!

All of her border difficulties manifested themselves in difficulties with eating and dieting, with a fixed idea about becoming thin and the fear of getting fat. These thoughts dominate her life during the last ten years. She diets wildly, then makes herself vomit to become thin, and in fact becomes quite skinny. Then she eats in wild orgies, bloating and becoming fat. The wild fluctuations in weight are attempts to establish her borders, to differentiate between outside and inside. But none of it works because historicity fails her.

The difficulty and expense of anxiety management and its failure are well recorded in her diary and other writings. When she was seventeen she wrote a poem, "I Hate You." In it she sings of a boy supremely beautiful, whom she now hates, because of his victorious smile, just as intensely as she had formerly loved him. She cannot stand that she is so tired and he is not. In another poem, "Tired," she talks of the grey damp evening mist which wells up around her and stretches out its arms toward the cold, long-diseased heart; while the trees shake their heads in disconsolate gloom, singing an old mournful song, no bird lets its late song be heard; no light appears in the sky; her head is empty and her heart is afraid.

The emptiness that is part of the failure of historicity adds to the feeling of anxiety and must be mentioned as a constant companion of schizophrenic existence. Because of the failure of historicity there is no track record for anxiety management, no patterns of management readily available to recall; no personality has developed to serve as an automated source of inexpensive management of dread and fear. Each time during the thousands of times in the day that anxiety wells up and fear and dread overwhelm, the existence must start from scratch to find a way to hold on, and hope is not available because not only is the past not there but the future is not suspected. The existence is a victim of the present moment, like a decerebrate preparation for stimulus response demonstration.

Over and over again Ellen West expresses the tiredness of managing anxiety. When she was eighteen years old she visited Paris and wrote in her diary the praises of great enthusiasm about everything true and beautiful she had experienced while on this trip with her parents.

At twenty-one she wrote:

> Now death no longer appears to be as terrible; death is not a man with the scythe but a glorious woman, white asters in her dark hair, large eyes, dream-deep and grey.

The only thing which still lures her is dying:

> Such a delicious stretching out and dozing off. Then it's over. No more getting up and dreary working and planning. Back of every word I really hide a yawn.

In a letter to a male friend she writes:

> And every day I get a little fatter, older, and uglier.

In these words we see not only her difficulty with historicity which makes her question her borders and body image, not only her difficulty with being worn out and tired from ineffectively and expensively managing her anxiety, but also the difficulty with self-esteem which then secondarily results in the terribly impaired interpersonal relationship. She goes on to write to the same friend:

> If he makes me wait much longer, the great friend, death, then I shall set out and seek him.

At the same time she also writes that she is not melancholy but merely tired, worn out, and apathetic:

> Everything is so uniform to me, so utterly indifferent, I know no feeling of joy and none of fear.

> Death is the greatest happiness in life, if not the only one. Without hope of the end, life would be unendurable. Only the certainty that sooner or later the end must come consoles me a little.

Ellen West goes on to write in her diary:

> The murderer must feel somewhat as I do, who constantly sees in his mind's eye the picture of the victim. He can work, even slave, from early until late, he can go out, can talk, can attempt to divert himself: all in vain. Always and always again he will see the picture of the victim before him. He feels an overpowering pull toward the place of the murder. He knows that this makes him suspect. Even worse—he has a horror of that place, but still he must go there. Something that is stronger than his reason and his will controls him and makes of his life a frightful scene of devastation. The murderer can find redemption. He goes to the police and accuses himself. In the punishment he atones for his crime. I can find no redemption—except in death.

Somewhat later, near the end of her life, she writes to her husband Karl:

> Ask a prisoner of war some time whether he would rather stay in the prison camp or return to his homeland. In the prison camp he studies foreign languages and concerns himself with this or that; of course, only to *help* himself get over the long, hard days. Does he really enjoy the work? Would he for its sake remain in prison camp even a minute longer than necessary? Certainly not, and nobody will even dream up such a grotesque idea. But of me it is required. Life has become a prison camp for me, and I long as ardently for death as the poor soldier in Siberia longs for his homeland.
>
> The comparison with imprisonment is no play on words. I am in prison, caught in a net from which I cannot free myself. I am a prisoner within myself; I get more and more entangled, and every day is a new, useless struggle; the meshes tighten more and more. I am in Siberia; my heart is icebound, all around me is solitude and cold. My best days are a sadly comic attempt to deceive myself as to my true condition. It is undignified to live on like this. Karl, if you love me, grant me death.
>
> I am surrounded by enemies. Wherever I turn, a man stands there with sword drawn. As on the stage: the unhappy one rushes toward the exit; stop! An armed man confronts him. He rushes to a second, to a third exit. All in vain. He is surrounded, he can no longer get out. He collapses in despair.
>
> So it is with me: I am in prison and cannot get out. It does no good for the analyst to tell me that I myself place the armed men there, that they are theatrical figments and not real. *To me they are very real.*

The third primary difficulty in the life of schizophrenic existence is the pain and agony of interpersonal transactions. From each of these the existence comes back more tired, more in self-doubt, less in hope of relating to others. From each human transaction, no matter how good or bad—in fact, quite independently of the actual outcome of the transaction—the schizophrenic existence feels somewhat worse about itself. We hear this in the words of Ellen West:

I am withdrawing more and more from people. I feel myself excluded from all real life. I am quite isolated. I sit in a glass ball. I see people through a glass wall, their voices come to be muffled. I have an unutterable longing to get to them. I scream, but they do not hear me. I stretch out my arms toward them; but my hands merely beat against the walls of my glass ball.

She expresses this in other poems:

> I'd like to die just as the birdling does
> That splits his throat in highest jublilation;
> And not to live as the worm on earth lives on,
> Becoming old and ugly, dull and dumb!
> No, feel for once how forces in me kindle,
> And wildly be consumed in my own fire.

> Woe's me, woe's me!
> The earth bears grain,
> But I
> Am unfruitful,
> Am discarded shell,
> Cracked, unusable,
> Worthless husk.
> Creator, creator,
> Take me back!
> Create me a second time
> And create me better!

As a result of the agony and pain of managing anxiety so expensively and managing the interpersonal transactions so painfully, schizophrenic existence always ends up with a fragile, low, and impaired self-esteem and self-idea. The difficulty with self-esteem in schizophrenic existence, which is secondary to all three of the primary categories of difficulty—the lack of historicity, the expense and ineffectiveness of anxiety management, and the pain and negative outcome of interpersonal transactions—is almost always present. Yet it is clear, when we follow Sydenham's advice and go back to the patient (as we did with Ellen West), that even the impaired self-esteem is secondary to the three fundamental categories of phenomena that are part of every schizophrenic existence.

Ellen West writes about interpersonal danger and the tragic outcome. In a poem written during her seventeenth year, entitled "Kiss Me Dead," she asks:

> Is there no rescue anymore?

She calls upon the cold, grim Sea King to come to her, take her in his arms in ardent love-lust, and kiss her to death.

All interpersonal transactions must end in death, in her nonexistence. Because she lacks the historicity which could remind her that she had survived interpersonal transactions in the past, each one consumes her totally. There is nothing left except the emptiness with which she began.

A THEORETICAL FORMULATION OF SCHIZOPHRENIC EXISTENCE—A THEORY OF PATHOLOGY

We have begun our study of schizophrenia with the observations of the existence of itself. We have looked at our observations of ourself in juxtaposition to the schizophrenic existence, and finally we have recorded our observation of schizophrenic life style in action. These observations and experiences have led me to the conclusion that there are three *primary* phenomena that are seen in all schizophrenic existences: (1) the *failure of historicity;* (2) the *expensive* and *ineffective management of anxiety;* and (3) the disastrously *painful interpersonal transactions.* The failure of historicity is somewhat basic to the other two primary defects. The failure of historicity can help us to understand some aspects of the difficulty with anxiety management and some of the difficulty in the interpersonal transactions. However, a part of the difficulty with anxiety management and interpersonal transaction pain must be understood as being independent of the difficulty with historicity.

All other observations of schizophrenic existence are secondary to these primary categories of phenomena. The first layer of secondary phenomena includes the feelings of emptiness and nothingness which are secondary to difficulty with historicity. The difficulty

CATEGORIES OF OBSERVED EXISTENTIAL DIFFICULTIES IN SCHIZOPHRENIC LIFE STYLE

Primary	Secondary	Tertiary	Quaternary
Failure of historicity (Basic)*	Feelings of emptiness and nothingness	Autism	Filling with food, activity
		Affective difficulty	Suicidal behavior
Expense and failure of anxiety management	Impaired self-esteem		Megalomania and delusions of grandeur
Pain and failure of interpersonal transactions	No past, no future, no flow of time	Ambivalence	
		Difficulty with ego boundaries and body image	Physical clumsiness
	Tiredness and exhaustion		
		Failure to learn from experience	Ritualistic behavior
	Loose association in the presence of "normal" anxiety		Hypochondriasis
		Hopelessness	
			Delusions
	Dread and fear	Confusion	Hallucinations
	Fragility of adjustment	Enslavement in the present movement of action	Crazy behavior
	Fragile integrity of personality		Paranoia
	Withdrawal		Polymorphous sexuality
			Impaired reality testing

* This category seems to play a part in all of the other difficulties of schizophrenic existence.

with "ego boundaries," with body image, is also partially the result of failure of historicity. The difficulty of the impaired self-esteem is the result of all three of the primary difficulties. The clumsy interpersonal transactions from which the existence comes away feeling worse about himself further contributes to low self-esteem. Expensive and ineffective anxiety management contributes even further. The hopelessness results from the secondary defect of the closed future seen in schizophrenic existence, which in turn is based upon the primary defect of historicity. The difficulty in the flow of time, the nonavailability of past, the impossibility of relying on the future or even fantasying the future, makes the schizophrenic existence a victim of the present.

The traditional "Four A's" of Bleuler are the result of the three primary categories of observed phenomena. We know that logical errors, such as loose associations, occur in all people when they are very anxious. They're seen on test papers among students; they are seen in each of us in our thinking during periods of high levels of anxiety, dread, and fear. Since the schizophrenic existence cannot manage anxiety but tires easily from even minimal anxiety management, it always lives with a chronically high head of free-floating, unbound, unmanaged, or improperly managed anxiety. The difference between the schizophrenic existence and the nonschizophrenic existence is not the presence of a thought difficulty—sometimes called loose associations—but the difficulty in anxiety management which makes the schizophrenic existence so anxious that its associations are much more frequently loose than those of the nonschizophrenic existence.

The autism described by Bleuler, withdrawal from the world and the predominance of the internal world, is the result of the primary difficulty with historicity which makes it impossible to maintain ego boundaries and to differentiate between inside and outside. It is also the result of the difficulty of anxiety management which leaves the schizophrenic existence tired, worn out, and unable to respond. And thirdly, it is related to the tragic and painful interpersonal transactions which make the schizophrenic existence give up and withdraw from interpersonal space like a snail withdraws into its shell.

The affective difficulty which Bleuler describes as flat and inappropriate, but which most clinicians today would describe as mercurial and wild, is also secondary to the basic difficulty of having no historicity. Furthermore, the affective phenomena are influenced by the difficulty with anxiety management and the difficulty in the interpersonal space. We learn much of the affective response in the interpersonal space, and this is not learned by the schizophrenic existence because that avenue is not available.

The fourth observation of Bleuler's—the immobilizing ambivalence—must also be attributed to the failure of historicity. Ambivalence is part of the human condition, but the ambivalence of the nonschizophrenic existence can be resolved. The schizophrenic existence gets stuck between the two opposing poles, between the wanting and not wanting, the wishing and hating. It is here that the failure of historicity manifests itself so clearly when the existence can take no risks and make no decisions in any direction.

In summary, then, the secondary difficulties include impaired self-esteem, the emptiness, the nothingness, the tiredness, the withdrawal, and the constantly painful and unmanageable dread, fear, and anxiety. The secondary difficulties also include the victimization of the schizophrenic existence by the present, and the failure of the influence of the past and future on the existence.

The third level of difficulties of the schizophrenic existence includes the difficulties with ego boundaries and self-borders, the difficulties with body image, the immobilizing ambivalence, and the loose associations resulting in idiosyncratic logic. Also included are the feelings of hopelessness and failure to learn from experience, the need to function as a slave of the present, and the emptiness and fragility of interpersonal relationships. This third category also includes the autism and the immobilizing ambivalence.

The fourth-level category of phenomena includes the clinical observations in the medical model of schizophrenia, that is, the delusions, hallucinations, the catatonic states, and the pathetic silliness of the misshapen management of anxiety in the hebephrenic, and the paranoid projections and the ritualistic behavior of the chronic schizophrenic patient. Clinical symptoms are best understood if we remember that they are attempts at restitution. The three primary

defects result in the painfully low self-esteem, the terrible emptiness, the dreadful loneliness, the frightening anxiety. No one can
live with such painful symptoms. The person attempts to restitute
for these defects in order to lessen the agony. Delusions of grandeur
are restitution for low self-esteem. Hallucinations fill the emptiness.
Delusions bind anxiety by denial and projection. Rituals fill emptiness. Hypochondriasis focuses on body image and self-borders. Poly-
morphous sexuality restitutes for lack of intimate human relationships.

It follows that if the primary difficulties with anxiety, historicity,
and interpersonal transactions are managed and repaired, then the
person can give up the "symptoms" of schizophrenic existence.
And, indeed, that is exactly what happens. In clinical psychiatry,
symptoms can be suppressed with medication or environmental ma-
nipulations. Symptoms can also be made unnecessary if the patient
is helped to find healthier ways of restituting. From our phenomenological theory of schizophrenia, a logical and consistent approach
to helping can be developed.

A LOGICAL APPROACH TO THE
HELPING INTERVENTION

Now that we have a theoretical formulation of schizophrenic existence, based on a detailed analysis of observed verbal and nonverbal
phenomena of schizophrenic life style and a system of categories in
which to organize these observed phenomena, we are ready to develop a logical approach to the helping intervention. The tremendous difficulty in intervening in a helpful way in schizophrenic existence is exemplified in the case of Ellen West. Perhaps we might
begin by raising the question of whether a nonschizophrenic existence has the right or perhaps the duty to intervene in alleviating the
distress and terror of the schizophrenic existence. In order to answer that question we must ask whether we can intervene in a useful way and what the outcome of such intervention will be.

Let me quote from the last two notes in the hospital chart of Ellen West in a Swiss sanitarium, where Professor Ludwig Binswanger was the therapist.

(March 24th)

(Consultation with Professor E. Bleuler
and a German psychiatrist.)

The preliminaries of this consultation are as follows:

In view of the increasing risk of suicide, continued residence of the patient on the open ward could not be justified. I had to put before her husband the alternative of giving permission to transfer his wife to closed ward, or leaving the institution with her. The very reasonable husband saw my point perfectly clearly, but said he could give his permission for the closed ward only if a cure or at least a far-reaching improvement of his wife could be promised. Since on the basis of the anamnesis and my own observations I had to diagnose a progressive schizophrenic psychosis (schizophrenia simplex), I could offer the husband very little hope. Since it was clear that her release from the institution meant certain suicide, I had to advise the husband in the light of this responsibility not to rely upon my opinion alone —certain as I was of my case—but to arrange for consultation with Professor Bleuler on the one hand, and on the other hand with another psychiatrist whose views were not too close to the Kraepelin-Bleuler theory of schizophrenia. The complete anamnesis, as well as our case record, was handed to the consultants in advance of their interviews with the patient.

Result of the consultation: Both gentlemen agreed completely with my prognosis and doubt any therapeutic usefulness of commitment even more emphatically than I. For Bleuler, the presence of schizophrenia is indubitable. The second psychiatrist declared that schizophrenia can be diagnosed only if an intellectual defect exists. In our case he would label it a psychopathic constitution which was progressively unfolding. All three of us agreed that it is not a case of obsessional neurosis and not one of manic-depressive psychosis and that no definitely reliable therapy is possible. We therefore resolved to give in to the patient's demand for discharge.

(March 30th)

The patient was visibly relieved by the result of the consultation. She declared that she would now take her life into her own hands, but was much shaken when she saw that despite her best intentions she could not master her dilemma with regard to her overeating and her excessive and bizarre dieting. Externally she controlled herself powerfully and was quiet and orderly, but inwardly she was very tense and agitated. She pondered this way and that what she could do now, and finally resolved to leave the sanitarium with her husband this very day. She continued precisely her whole way of life until the last, since every change "confuses her and throws her completely off the track." She was tormented in the extreme by her "idea," her wish to be thin but her inability to keep herself from stuffing herself with food to fill the emptiness up to the last moment. Weight upon leaving, approximately the same as upon arriving at the hospital; namely, 104 pounds.

Binswanger's account continues:

On her trip home Ellen is very courageous. The reason for taking the trip gives her strength. The glimpse into life which the trip gives her, hurts her. Even more than in the institution, she feels incapable of dealing with life. The following days are more harrowing than all the previous weeks. She feels no release of tension; on the contrary, all of her symptoms appear more strongly. The irregularity of her way of life upsets her completely; the reunion with her relatives only brings her illness more clearly into view. On the third day of being home she is as if transformed. At breakfast she eats butter and sugar. At noon she eats so much that for the first time in 13 years she is satisfied by her food and feels really full. Later, at the afternoon coffee hour, she eats chocolate cream and Easter eggs. She takes a walk with her husband, reads poems by Rilke, Storm, Goethe, and Tennyson. She is amused by the first chapter of Mark Twain's "Christian Science." She is in a positively festive mood and all heaviness seems to have fallen away from her. She writes letters, the last one is a letter to a fellow patient at the sanitarium to whom she had become attached. In the evening she takes a lethal dose of poison and on the following morning she is dead. She looked as she had never looked in life—calm and happy and peaceful.

Thus ended the case of Ellen West fifty years ago. She was given the best medical interventions available at that time. Today, in 1973, I am not at all sure that the outcome—with the best medical model interventions, including medication, milieu therapy, or prolonged locking-up in a "hospital"—would be any different.[15]

However, the case raises important questions for us. These questions fall into two categories: those of philosophy and those of technique.

There has been a great deal of philosophical discussion about the question of the helping intervention in schizophrenic existence. This becomes a particular issue in the medical model. Does one have the right to interfere in the life of another for purposes of preventing suicide and prolonging pain and agony? Does one have the right to impose consensually validated reality on idiosyncratic reality? Does one have the duty or right to treat when treatment hasn't been requested and in fact is resisted? Is it philosophically justified to treat someone or to intervene in his life because he doesn't fit into the life style of the majority culture or the majority culture calls him sick? Or is the opposite justified—as in the case of Ellen West? Should someone be allowed to commit suicide if he chooses to?

One of the major criticisms leveled at the existential approach has been the relative nonaggressiveness in pursuing the treatment process, as, for example, in the case of Ellen West. I do not wish to elaborate here in detail on all aspects of such a discussion since these points of view have been well represented in the literature.[16] The medical model tends to insist that "treatment" interventions are the duty of every physician at all times, regardless of what sense they make, regardless of the civil rights of the treatment object (or victim). The opposite view insists that, above all else, the civil rights of every living human being must be preserved and no treatment can ever be an excuse for any imposed intervention forced on any existence. Between these two extreme philosophical positions, a variety of attitudes can resolve the question. The key to resolving the issue is consideration of the ability of the person to judge and make judgments, to evaluate reality, and to take responsibility. When the educational and social models are used, the same questions come up in different metaphors—for example, who has the primary right: the individual existence, the family, society, humanity?

Also, my purpose here is not to go into the details or techniques of intervention—all this has been discussed in many other papers and books.[17] The literature attests to a multitude of approaches to the treatment intervention. A review of the literature shows that the many theories and many interventions make little difference. What seems to make the difference is the transaction which occurs between schizophrenic existence and other existences. Once the intervention transactions are related to the understanding of the three primary existential categories of difficulties, that is, the failure of historicity, the difficulty with anxiety management, the painfulness of interpersonal relationships, it becomes perfectly clear why theories of the therapist matter little and why many different theories and techniques of intervention have the same outcome.[18]

If the primary existential difficulties are dealt with in the helping interventions, all else seems to fall into place—as indeed one would expect from this theory and understanding of schizophrenic existence. The secondary, tertiary, and quaternary levels of difficulties and stumbling blocks of existence, which are directly related to the three primary ones and, most importantly, to the basic difficulty with historicity, seem to be resolved if the interventions deal with the primary existential difficulties. When these three are dealt with, the other difficulties show relief, change, and improvement.

Since all interventions in the existence are based on the relationship of one existence with another, and since we have already mentioned in considerable detail that a major difficulty in the schizophrenic existence is in the interpersonal sphere, it becomes clear that the difficulty of intervention is great. One of the very aspects of existence that is most difficult for a schizophrenic life style must also become the vehicle for rescue, for relief of distress, and for change; that is, an interpersonal relationship between a schizophrenic existence and another must occur and must become the vehicle for the lifeline of helping transactions.

Due to the failure of historicity, the patient is imprisoned in the present moment. One of the most useful interventions is to reopen the future and to make available the past. In other words, in the relationship between the existence and the helping other and the rest of the world, the flow of time from past and future into present which has stopped must be restarted. The schizophrenic existence must have an opportunity for the experience of time, knowing some past and future through the present. Even though at the beginning this may simply be from one hour to the next, it is possible to intervene in such a way that the whole world of remembering, of having been, of being and acting, and of anticipating and expecting, can be *opened*. This is done in the structure of the new relationship. The techniques are many, but essentially consist of meticulous attention by the other to demonstrate his reliability, his scrupulous care in the keeping of appointments, his life-and-death struggle in being reliable, his careful and considerate attention to the minutae and details of interpersonal transactions. To open the doors of the existential prison of the present by making available the immediate past and the immediate future in the helping transaction, the intervening other must provide a corrective emotional experience which attempts to open the flow of time. It is possible to slowly stretch out the past and the future to the more remote past and remote future. The establishment of time flow into the present, and thus the establishment of anticipatory affect, as well as memory affect, can be established by such simple techniques as planning, remembering, validating, and experiencing together and then immediately talking about it. The repeated experience of a schizophrenic existence—hearing from another, "I will see you tomorrow at ten o'clock"—may be the most useful helping intervention in the establishment of historicity and in developing an openness to both past and future. Obviously, for that promise to have the effect of a corrective emotional experience, it must be kept scrupulously—and always, not once, not one hundred times, but forever. Because of the fragility of the flow of time established in the schizophrenic existence, with its ever-present difficulty with historicity, unreliability is intolerable even after years of reliability. It is for this reason that the helping interventions fail most often. The helper fails to remember the difficulty the schizophrenic existence has with time flow—particularly when the secondary and tertiary signs and symptoms are not clearly visible at the moment. The result is usually an immediate disaster. The schizophrenic existence loses the relationship, historicity is stuck once more, and it is as though the relationship had never been. In the dualities of the helping transaction between the schizophrenic existence and the other, the establishment of the flow of time becomes pivotal. It is done through the multitude of transactions which must demonstrate reliability, consistency, attention to detail, and continuity far into the future. Termination of the transaction at any time may result in the closing down of the flow of time once again, as though the experiences of the transaction had never occurred. The most common cause of failure of the helping intervention is loss of interest in its continuing by the other.

The problems with anxiety management in the schizophrenic existence are many. Helpful interventions can be made in a multitude of ways. Traditionally, within the medical model, the administering of medication lowers the awareness of anxiety in the schizophrenic existence and therefore allows the person to be less overwhelmed by his anxiety management efforts. In the interpersonal sphere, anxiety management can be aided by teaching the schizophrenic existence some simple techniques of avoiding anxiety-producing situations and by developing techniques for coping. The teaching of these techniques must be based on a thorough understanding of the difficulties of all schizophrenic existence. Yet the choice of techniques for each schizophrenic life style must be based on thorough and detailed understanding of each specific schizophrenic existence. Anxiety management techniques which have worked for a particular existence in the past, as well as new techniques based on detailed individual knowledge, can be part of the repertoire.

The helping other must allow the schizophrenic existence to be unique and different from him. This attitude must be monitored even though the schizophrenic existence is so eager to fill his emptiness by imitating the helping other in all details. This attempt at self-filling should not be discouraged; rather, it should be recognized as a temporary splint for the schizophrenic personality which will lead to ultimate failure. Above all, the helper must help the schizophrenic existence avoid another failure in the interpersonal space, particularly in the helping transaction. In helping, we must also always be aware that one schizophrenic existence is no more like another schizophrenic existence than one helping other is like another helping other. Observations in categories of phenomenology have only limited value as a form of summarizing our observations. These classifications gloss over the individual differences of each existence and each life style.

When the schizophrenic existence is helped to develop some techniques of anxiety management, the results are dramatic. The so-called symptoms of schizophrenia almost disappear. The immobilizing ambivalence is relieved; the thought disorder (loose associations) no longer is clearly evident and does not interfere in the life style. The autism is interrupted, and it looks as though the existence once again turns its attention to the outside world. The affect and mood fluctuation begins to look less "flat"—in reality, less mercurial, and therefore less inhibited and constrained. In response to the decreased mercurial fluctuations, the affect even seems more appropriate to the thought content. The restitutive phenomena of hallucinations and delusions disappear. When the schizophrenic existence no longer needs to deal with the high level of anxiety for which the person has no tools of management and against which he cannot defend himself, all the symptoms seem to disappear. For this reason the modern drugs which decrease the awareness of the anxiety have been thought to be specific medications that "cure" schizophrenia almost as though they eradicated the schizococcus, that mythical cause of this disease.

The teaching of anxiety management techniques must occur in the interpersonal transaction. Some of the teaching is done by example, some of it by cognitive learning, and some by specific instructions of the helping other to the schizophrenic existence for the management of life situations. However, none of this works unless the issue of historicity has been adequately dealt with in the continuity of the interpersonal relationship. The flow of lived and experienced time has to be restarted first.

I have already mentioned that the interpersonal failure is most difficult to repair. Without establishing the relationship with the significant other, there is no input into the schizophrenic existence. Help and rescue are possible only through the avenue of the *inter*personal space. In the *intra*personal space of the world of schizophrenia there is only chaos and pain, isolation and misery, dread, fear, and emptiness. It is precisely in the area of establishing interpersonal relationships that personal style of helping is most evident. This leads to major differences in techniques of helping. These techniques vary from empathic tolerance of "being crazy," through wildly acting out demands for giving up one kind of craziness for another, to attempting to destroy the schizophrenic existence in favor of zombie-like, "as if" personality, to giving explanations to the schizophrenic existence, to glorifying schizophrenic life style. Any of these personal styles of helping can be a useful vehicle as long as the basic defects of schizophrenic existence are dealt with and as long as the type of helping meets the needs of the particular schizophrenic existence who is being helped rather than only the needs of the helper.

Establishment of an interpersonal relationship is extremely difficult. It requires great interest and patience by the helping other to attempt to throw a lifeline to the schizophrenic existence. However, once the relationship has been established, once anxiety management and the flow of historicity have been started, there can be dramatic relief of agony, dread, and pain. Through the interpersonal lifeline the border for the schizophrenic existence can be established and maintained. The secondary symptoms of Bleuler's "Four A's" can be altered, the emptiness can be partially filled, and self-esteem can be bolstered.

Thus, when the helping transaction is looked at as related to the three fundamental categories of phenomena of difficulties described and developed in this approach to an understanding of schizophrenic existence, observations we have made in the past begin to make sense.

SUMMARY

The schizophrenic existence, its unique life style and its state of agony, can be understood. Helping interventions can be made even though the "cause" remains obscure as long as the helping interventions are related to the categories of observed phenomena of difficulties in schizophrenic existence. At this point in our understanding of existence neither the genetic, nor the biochemical, nor the interpersonal, nor the social theories seem to offer adequate understanding of schizophrenic life style by themselves. Rather, each of these seems to be only one link in the chain of events which leads to schizophrenic existence as we know it today. There is no evidence today that biochemical changes cause schizophrenia any more than there is evidence that schizophrenia causes biochemical changes. The same can be said for the interpersonal and social theories of etiology. But even without knowing "the cause" or "multitude of causes," it is possible to understand schizophrenic existence and to develop a rational and effective strategy for helping based on this understanding.

NOTES

[1] These writings and words of patients have been collected by the author in the course of twenty years of clinical practice. Some of them were published in *The Therapeutic Management of Psychological Illness,* by Werner M. Mendel and Gerald A. Green. New York: Basic Books, Inc., 1967.

[2] Fascinating details of the history of mental illness in Mesopotamia, Egypt, among the ancient Hebrews, and in early Chinese history can be found in chapter 3, "Contributions of the Ancients," in *The History of Psychiatry,* by Franz G. Alexander and Sheldon T. Selesnick. New York: Harper & Row, 1966, pp. 17–26.

[3] This term was first proposed by Franz Alexander to describe certain aspects of the therapy transaction. The *corrective emotional experience* is a useful concept in attempting to understand how therapy

works. See Franz Alexander, *Psychoanalysis and Psychotherapy*. New York: W. W. Norton, 1956.

⁴ Dr. Helene Deutsch developed the concept of the "as if" personality to describe the borrowed healthy façade which the schizophrenic person can use to appear healthy and to function nearly normally. See "Some Forms of Emotional Disturbance and Their Relationship to Schizophrenia, *Psychoanalytic Quarterly*, 11:301, 1942.

⁵ Hans Selye developed the concept of diseases of adaptation. *The Physiology and Pathology of Exposure to Stress*. Montreal: ACTA, 1950.

⁶ This view was developed in the many writings of Stewart Wolf and Harold Wolff. An early example of this approach is found in the paper "Evidence of the Genesis of Peptic Ulcer in Man," J.A.M.A., 120:670, 1942.

⁷ Eugen Bleuler, *Dementia Praecox or the Group of Schizophrenias*. New York: International Universities Press, 1950.

⁸ Martin Buber, *Tales of the Hasidim: The Early Masters*. New York: Schocken Books, Inc., 1947 (paperback).

⁹ Thomas Sydenham (1624–1689), an English physician and medical teacher.

¹⁰ Eugene Minkowski, *Le temps vecu*. Paris: D'Artrey, 1933.

¹¹ Erwin Straus, "The Upright Posture," *Psychiatric Quarterly*, 26:529, October 1952.

¹² Werner M. Mendel and Murray Wexler, "Perceptual Organization of Schizophrenic Patients," *Existential Psychiatry*, 6:22:145, 1967.

¹³ Dr. Harry Stack Sullivan felt that the low self-esteem was the basic phenomenon of schizophrenia which could explain all other findings and all symptoms. *The Interpersonal Theory of Psychiatry*. New York: W. W. Norton, 1953.

¹⁴ "Der Fall Ellen West," *Schweizer Archiv für Neurologie und Psychiatrie*, 1944, vol. 53, pp. 255–277; vol. 54, pp. 69–117, 330–360; 1945, vol. 55, pp. 16–40.

¹⁵ The problem of hospitalization has been discussed in "Effect of Length of Hospitalization on Rate and Quality of Remission from Acute Psychotic Episodes," *Journal of Nervous and Mental Diseases*, 143:226, 1966; in "On the Abolition of the Psychiatric Hospital (chapter 11, pp. 237–247), in *Comprehensive Mental Health*, Madison: The University of Wisconsin Press, 1968, written by the author; and in other papers by the author.

¹⁶ Franz Alexander, *The Western Mind in Transition*. New York: Random House, 1960, chapter XI, "Existentialism and Psychoanalysis."

[17] Werner M. Mendel (with Gerald A. Green), *The Therapeutic Management of Psychological Illness.* New York: Basic Books, Inc., 1967; Mendel, "The Future in the Model of Psychopathology," *Journal of Existential Psychiatry,* 1:27, 1961; Mendel, "Structure as Process in Psychotherapy," *Journal of Existential Psychiatry,* 4:301, 1964; Mendel and Samuel Rapport, "Outpatient Treatment for Chronic Schizophrenic Patients," *Archives of General Psychiatry,* 8:190, 1963; Mendel, "Non-specifics of Psychotherapy," *International Journal of Psychiatry,* 5:5:400, 1968.

[18] Compare the theoretical differences in the approach of Freida Fromm-Reichmann, *Psychoanalysis and Psychotherapy: Selected Papers of Freida Fromm-Reichmann,* Chicago: University of Chicago Press, 1959; John Rosen, *Direct Analysis: Selected Papers,* New York: Grune & Stratton, 1953; Harold Searles, *Collected Papers on Schizophrenia,* New York: International Universities Press, 1965; Harry Stack Sullivan, *The Interpersonal Theory of Psychiatry,* New York: Norton, 1953; *Clinical Studies in Psychiatry,* New York: Norton, 1956; *Schizophrenia as a Human Process,* New York: Norton, 1962; Otto Will, Jr., "Process, Psychotherapy and Schizophrenia," in *Psychotherapy of the Psychoses,* A. Burton (Ed.), New York: Basic Books, Inc., 1961; and Werner M. Mendel (with Gerald A. Green), *The Therapeutic Management of Psychological Illness,* New York: Basic Books, 1967.

All of these therapists look at the treatment process from a very different theoretical point of view, yet basically they all have good results. Perhaps this can be understood only if we recognize that different therapists use a different metaphor for treatment but, in fact, do very similar things. All pay meticulous, concerned attention to the details of the patient's life, and they spend a great deal of energy and time in the relationship to the patient. The content (words) of the therapy transaction seems to matter little. The process (interactional behavior) of the transaction seems all-important.

INDEX